MW00398616

The Pequot War

A Captivating Guide to the Armed Conflict in New England between the Pequot People and English Settlers and Its Role in the History of the United States of America

© Copyright 2020

All Rights Reserved. No part of this book may be reproduced in any form without permission in writing from the author. Reviewers may quote brief passages in reviews.

Disclaimer: No part of this publication may be reproduced or transmitted in any form or by any means, mechanical or electronic, including photocopying or recording, or by any information storage and retrieval system, or transmitted by email without permission in writing from the publisher.

While all attempts have been made to verify the information provided in this publication, neither the author nor the publisher assumes any responsibility for errors, omissions or contrary interpretations of the subject matter herein.

This book is for entertainment purposes only. The views expressed are those of the author alone, and should not be taken as expert instruction or commands. The reader is responsible for his or her own actions.

Adherence to all applicable laws and regulations, including international, federal, state and local laws governing professional licensing, business practices, advertising and all other aspects of doing business in the US, Canada, UK or any other jurisdiction is the sole responsibility of the purchaser or reader.

Neither the author nor the publisher assumes any responsibility or liability whatsoever on the behalf of the purchaser or reader of these materials. Any perceived slight of any individual or organization is purely unintentional.

Free Bonus from Captivating History
(Available for a Limited time)

Hi History Lovers!

Now you have a chance to join our exclusive history list so you can get your first history ebook for free as well as discounts and a potential to get more history books for free! Simply visit the link below to join.

Captivatinghistory.com/ebook

Also, make sure to follow us on Facebook, Twitter and Youtube by searching for Captivating History.

Contents

Introduction

The Pequot War (1636–1638) was a short-lived but extremely violent and bloody episode in United States history. This event represents one of the turning points in the entire history of North America, as the war changed the balance of power. The Dutch colonial authorities lost their status of being the dominant economic and political force, while the English took over this epithet. The end of the war also represented the first stage in England's intensive expansion in that part of the world.

This historical event demonstrates the insurmountable antagonisms between two opposing cultures and perceptions. It was just the beginning of the conflicts between the European settlers and the Native Americans, as the Pequot War allowed the Puritans to have a testing ground so they could examine their military capabilities in the New World and observe the capabilities of the Native American tribes.

The book is composed of several chapters that examine various aspects of the Pequot War. In the beginning, the reader will have the opportunity to get acquainted with the Europeans' views on the people who inhabited the New World. The average European image of the indigenous "savage" who lived in North America is one of the key elements essential for understanding the enormous amount of violence recorded during the Pequot War, as well as other conflicts that later took place. In this book, one can also find information on the Pequot tribe and their importance to the wider Connecticut area, as well as their customs, way of life, and religion. The conditions in which the Puritans left their homeland, the process of settlement and colonization, the organization of the colonies, and the ambitions of the leaders of New England are also elaborated upon.

This conflict was the product of extremely complex events, and one of the broadest chapters of this paper talks about the events that led to the war. This book also provides details about the military capabilities of the warring parties. Both sides' combat tactics are presented in detail, including the military arsenal that the Puritans and Pequots had at their disposal. There will be an inside view of the military maneuvers, initial war operations, and conflicts between the warring parties. The central and most extensive part of the book talks about the organization of the largest military operation during the Pequot War: the English Mystic River campaign, which was also the conflict's final stage.

The Pequot War contains racial and religious issues that allude to the genocidal actions of Europeans in North America. This dimension of the war is still the subject of controversy among the academic community, and one will understand why. Finally, there will be a discussion of the consequences of the Pequot War and the historiographical approach to this event.

Throughout this book, we will expand our understanding of the main protagonists of this historical episode. These individuals made their mark on one of the most significant episodes in the history of the United States.

Chapter 1 – The European Conception of the Native Americans

Suppose we start looking for the factors that led to the Pequot War and other mutual conflicts between the Native Americans and Europeans. In that case, it is necessary to look at the European man's understanding of the indigenous tribes of North America. The earliest records of the newly discovered world and the natives of North America significantly led to the formation of stereotypes. These records depict Native Americans as blasphemous savages who drink blood and sacrifice boys. The partial occurrence of cannibalism among Native Americans had a considerably negative effect on the European understanding of the natives of North America, and texts about ghost worship and witchcraft had a very negative impact on Catholic Europeans. Records of incest, sodomy, and witchcraft are also common elements found in these early texts.

Intensive contact between Europeans and natives from the beginning of colonization led to the appearance of infectious diseases among North American natives, who had not developed immunity to certain illnesses, such as smallpox, tuberculosis, influenza, and malaria. Europeans viewed this pandemic through the prism of religion. Namely, the established opinion was that God was punishing the Native Americans for blasphemy and, in general, for their way of life, one that was unacceptable to Europeans. The Puritans believed that, in this way, God "purified" the earth for them and gave them space to settle. The Church also did not make any provisions for the Native Americans; on the contrary, the Church propagated Christianity among the natives at all costs. This ubiquitous view of Native Americans resonated among Puritans as well. It is undoubtedly one of the elements that led to the unprecedented brutality during the Pequot War.

From the beginning of the 17th century, the New World became synonymous with the incarnation of Satan. Because of such attitudes, it is not surprising that the Puritans were skeptical about coexisting with the Pequot and other tribes in the neighborhood. Information about such attitudes of the Puritans is brought to us by the Massachusetts Bay Colony's chronicler, Edward Johnson, who served as a soldier in the Pequot War and was one of the founders of Woburn, Massachusetts. Europeans believed that by colonizing, they brought peace and civilization to the Native Americans; however, the Europeans were, in fact, only imposing their politics, religion, economics, and universal understanding of life upon them. Europeans believed in moral superiority over others and sought to pass those values on to others at all costs.

Because of this European vision, Pequots and other American natives certainly aroused fear in the Europeans, and therefore, it was inevitable that the settlers would believe the natives posed a threat. One of the principles of the Puritan ideology of the time was the battle against evil. As mentioned above, the Native Americans were the devil incarnate, and the English believed that one of their main missions was to wage war against Satan. The English were also furious because their persistent efforts to baptize the native tribes were unsuccessful. The English colonists did not understand coexistence and tolerance, for they believed that if they allowed such a thing, in time, they would become such themselves.

Sadly, due to the lack of written sources, there is not much data on the Native American understanding of the Europeans. Apart from oral traditions, there are no other sources that tell us how they perceived Europeans and their ways. We know that the Native Americans at the beginning of colonization were pleased with their mutual trade cooperation. Through trade, Europeans introduced Native Americans to iron and specific technical achievements that made their daily lives more comfortable. Thus, the tribes developed good trade relations with the Dutch at the beginning of colonization and cooperated with them for years to the general satisfaction of all.

The problem arose when there was a mass migration of Europeans to North America. Disagreements arose among the European immigrants themselves, which greatly affected the indigenous population. According to the available oral traditions that have been preserved to this day, it is clear the Native Americans did not fully understand why the Europeans went to such lengths to impose their way of life upon the tribes. The natives observed the technological achievements of the more advanced European civilization with interest and curiosity. To them, the large European ships didn't look like boats; instead, the Native Americans called them "Moving Islands." It was not clear to Native Americans why Europeans wore so much clothing, given that they were mostly covering their intimate body parts. After arriving in North America, the first European researchers recorded how some natives began to worship metal axes and firearms after becoming acquainted with these objects. The Europeans' way of life and manners were utterly unknown to the natives, so these "white people with beards" were considered by some to be a new species. The interpretation of infectious diseases among the natives is also interesting; namely, they viewed this phenomenon as a terrible and deadly power that the white man carried with him.

Over time, the Native Americans began to view the Europeans as occupiers who wanted their country no matter the cost.

Chapter 2 – Who Were the Pequots?

The Pequots were a sizeable Native American tribe. According to the first historical sources dating back to 1600, the Pequot tribe had about 4,000 members. They inhabited the southeastern bank of the Connecticut River, as well as around the banks of the modern-day Thames River. The area they settled was about 250 square kilometers. According to the latest sources, the word "Pequot" comes from PAQUATAUOQ, WHICH LOOSELY TRANSLATES TO "destroyers." Most likely, that name was the product of fierce wars with other indigenous tribes. The Pequots were reputed to be aggressive and brave warriors. They are also believed to have migrated twenty years before the arrival of the English from the upper New York area.

Some believe their arrival in the Connecticut area was turbulent. It affected the entire region, as they displaced the smaller tribal communities that inhabited the area. By migrating, they showed their belligerent attitude toward others. However, this might not have been the case, as historical and scientific teachings regarding the migration of the Pequot tribe are quite divided. Some archaeological results indicate that the Pequot had inhibited the territory of Connecticut for much longer. Some linguistic studies also suggest a more established presence of the Pequot in the Connecticut area.

It is assumed that before the arrival of the Europeans, the Pequot was a community of clans. Each clan represented a different political entity, in which similar beliefs still prevailed. The establishment of trade relations with European immigrants changed certain social currents of the Pequot tribe. Before these first commercial connections, the Pequot tribe's dwellings were temporary. As their involvement in trade became more and more intense, the Native Americans became more attached to trading points and changed their nomadic habits. Under such circumstances, native settlements gained importance, as many became important trading places. To some extent, these economic changes affected the natives' attitude toward the environment, as the Pequots began to produce and exploit more natural resources.

In the early 17th century, the Pequot and Mohegan tribes were united, and they were led by Chief Sassacus. Soon, there was a split between these two tribes, and they began to act independently. Uncas, a former member of the unified Pequot tribe, separated with his like-minded people and formed the Mohegan tribe. Even though the Mohegans and the Pequots were identical in cultural characteristics, their different outlooks and interests in leadership led to the split between the two.

The Pequots engaged in agriculture, hunting, and fishing. The most important crops grown by this tribe were corn, beans, and pumpkins. It is interesting that women, with the help of children, were exclusively engaged in agriculture, except for the cultivation of tobacco, which was solely grown by men. The Pequots' diet was varied, although crops, meat, nuts, and fruits were regularly on the table.

The tribe lived in permanent dwellings, and during the hunting season, the men would leave their homes and form temporary settlements called "wigwams." These were shelters made of trees in a pyramidal shape, covered with tree bark, leaves, and animal skins.

The Pequots had an organized tribal hierarchy. The tribe's representative was the chief, but the shaman also had an important part in society. The tribal council played a pivotal role in decision-making. Between ten and fifteen men were on the council, and these men had to prove themselves in a certain way, whether on the battlefield or in another leadership role. The great chief, or sachem, was the most influential individual of the tribal community. The sachem's function oscillated according to the tribe, meaning that some sachems had greater and some lesser influence than others. As an interesting side note, women were equal members of Pequot society. They even had the right to run their own businesses.

The Pequots did not use money; instead, they relied on barter. Their trading currency was wampum, a highly coveted string of beads. This jewelry was not only a means of trade, as it also symbolized status in society and spiritual power. Wampum was valued not only by the Pequots but also by many other North American indigenous tribes. It should be noted the Pequots did not work for material gain. The notion of economic benefit did not exist; instead, the Pequots lived in the community and only used what natural resources they needed to survive.

The Pequots are generally known to have been extremely skilled hunters. The primary weapons used by the Pequots in both war and hunting were batons, axes, knives, and bows and arrows. They also used canoes made of wood for transport. The Pequots often deliberately caused controlled fires, thus maintaining the forests' passability, which made it easier for them to hunt. Before the Europeans' arrival on North American soil, the Pequots were already well organized in military, economic, and political terms. In primary sources, they mention the Pequots as a wealthy tribe compared to others.

The Pequots made their first contact with the Europeans at the end of the 15th and the beginning of the 16th century. Rigorous contact with the European immigrants continued during the 17th century, which was when the mass colonization of North America took place. The Pequots established intensive contact primarily with the Dutch, with whom the Pequots traded leather, decorative jewelry, and wampum. Like with many other indigenous tribes of North America, this more intense contact with Europeans was fatal to many. Namely, various contagious diseases were transmitted to them by the Europeans, decimating the tribes and somewhat changing the structure of North American tribal communities.

The beginning of the 17th century led to more mass migrations of European immigrants to North America, which led to an increase in the number of infected. The only way to fight infectious diseases was to leave the territory, after which the Europeans then seized the region for themselves. In 1616, in the area where the Massachusetts Bay Colony would be established later on, the bubonic plague broke out. The second wave of this disease occurred three years later, and it was even more intense than the first. In 1633 and 1634, an epidemic of smallpox occurred in the same area. These events greatly affected their native neighbors who were settled near the newly formed English colony, which was established in 1629. Among the closest were the Pequots. According to some sources, about 1,600 members of the Pequot tribe died from the bubonic plague and smallpox epidemics.

The interaction between the natives of North America and the Europeans had extremely tragic outcomes from the very beginning. The epidemics destroyed entire villages and families and attacked all sections of the population, including the Europeans. Although the Europeans had a higher immunity, 17th-century medicine was underdeveloped, which led to greater deaths. These diseases destroyed traditional social connections, especially in those tribal communities where the Europeans were in the "neighborhood." The coast of New England was very densely populated, and intensive trade contact between European immigrants and natives accelerated the spread of the epidemic. These epidemics were reported by English colonist Thomas Morton, whose account dates back to the 17th century. Morton is most notable for founding the colony of Merrymount, modern-day Quincy, Massachusetts. The Nauset tribe (also known as the Cape Cod Indians), who inhabited the Cape Cod area, captured a European colonist, who then transmitted the virus to the entire community. Morton writes the following about this event:

> One of these five men, outliving the rest, had learned so much of their language as to rebuke them for their bloody deed, saying that God would be angry with them for it, and that he would in his displeasure destroy them; but the savages (it seems boasting of their strength), replied and said, that they were so many that God could not kill them. But contrary-wise, in short time after the hand of God fell heavily upon them, with such a mortal stroke that they died on heaps as they lay in their houses; For in a place where many inhabited, there had been but one left to live to tell what became of the rest; the living being (as it seems) not able to bury the dead, they were left for crows, kites and vermin to prey upon. And the bones and skulls upon the several places of their habitations made such a spectacle after my coming into those parts, that, as I travelled in that forest near the Massachusetts, it seemed to me a new found Golgotha.

There is an obvious religious "overtone" in Morton's understanding of what occurred to the native tribe. This allows the reader to see how most of the Europeans observed the epidemics that raged against the native populace.

The elements of antagonism between European settlers and indigenous tribes were multiple, but one of the biggest barriers to mutual understanding was religion. Rigid Puritan beliefs were the biggest obstacle to any interaction between the natives of North America and the Europeans. The only fragment in which the two dogmatic narratives could be reconciled was the belief in the afterlife. The Native Americans, unlike Europeans, did not have colossal buildings intended for performing prayers or other forms of spiritual ritual. Religious symbols and texts were also not integral elements of the religious practices of the natives. The natives' religious beliefs were intertwined with their tradition, so fragments of their dogmatic beliefs permeated in their folklore. Through dance, the Native Americans sought to connect with the spiritual; it was one way in which they could become closer to a higher entity.

The Native American tribes that lived nearby the colonies of New England, among whom were the Pequots, believed the human soul existed on three levels. The first level of these beliefs involved people's spirits or souls. The Pequot believed that in certain states, the human soul separated from the body and could travel and communicate with the world around it. The second level implied guardian spirits; they, according to native beliefs, could exist in various forms and even take the forms of plants and animals. The highest degree implied a supreme entity, which could be compared to the Christian concept of God. As in many other religions, the Native Americans of North America believed in the intrusion of evil spirits (similar to Satan). Tribal shamans sought to drive such spirits out of the tribal community or reduce their appearance through various rituals.

The colonial census from 1774 showed about 151 members of the Pequot tribe on the Mashantucket Pequot Reservation, which is one of the oldest reservations in North America. The next census, which dates to the beginning of the 19th century, was even more devastating, as it showed only 35 members. By 1960, most Pequot on the reservation left for economic reasons. Those who remained were tied to the land of their ancestors. Local authorities sought to turn the Mashantucket Pequot Reservation into a state park. However, three half-sisters born and raised in the area, Alice Brend, Martha Langevin, and Elizabeth George, tried to obstruct this attempt at all costs. Thanks to their perseverance and efforts, and despite not having financial resources and adequate legal assistance, they managed to keep the reservation intact.

However, even during the 1970s, the situation was not significantly better, as the members of the reservation had many financial problems. During this period, the tribe survived on nature, their main food source, and minimal financial support. The tribal community also built a large greenhouse facility and raised domestic livestock. Today, the tribal community is governed by seven men over the age of fifty-five, who are elected for a term of three years. The tribal council manages all affairs but also maintains contacts with state and local representatives and authorities. Today, the tribal community takes special care of the youngest members of the community. Healthcare is regulated for everyone, and a significant emphasis is placed on education. The tribal community seeks to encourage as many people as possible to pursue higher education, no matter their age. The youngest community members learn about the history, culture, and traditions of the Pequot tribe.

Chapter 3 – The Massachusetts Bay Colony of New England

In the northeastern region of America, settlements were established in the early 17ᵗʰ century by two major religious groups: the Pilgrims and the Puritans. The Pilgrims settled the Atlantic coast in present-day Plymouth, Massachusetts. The Pilgrims were separatists from the Church of England, and they established Plymouth Colony in December of 1620, which was the first permanent European settlement in New England. It was also the second permanent settlement in North America, with Jamestown, Virginia, being the first. One of the major characters in this group of Pilgrims was William Bradford, who helped organize this venture for religious freedom. Bradford proved to be vital for the growth of Plymouth Colony because he, among others, helped frame the Mayflower Compact. The Mayflower Compact was the first governing document of Plymouth Colony, and it was also the first document of self-governance in the New World.

The other religious group to settle in America was the Puritans. Many Puritans first migrated to the Netherlands, but the liberal Dutch society was in complete contradiction to their beliefs. Therefore, they decided to move to the New World. The Puritans left England en masse, not only for religious reasons but also for economic ones.

There were two factions among the Puritans at the time: separatists and non-separatists. Separatist-minded Puritans believed that the Church was too corrupt and that reform was out of the question. In their opinion, the only solution was the complete separation from the Anglican Church. The other faction believed that an internal reorganization of the Church was possible. Such attitudes posed significant adversity among the Puritans. Namely, it was impossible to separate the Church from the state in England because that act would be considered high treason. Their only option was to leave their home country.

In 1628, John Endecott and a group of about 400 people and 200 cattle sailed to New England. At the time, it was one of the most participated overseas trips. When they arrived, John Endecott and other leaders founded the settlement of Naumkeag, which would later be renamed Salem. John Endecott was unofficially elected as the first governor of the newly formed colony. He would go on to become the longest-serving governor of the Massachusetts Bay Colony, serving for a total of sixteen years.

The Massachusetts Bay Colony was one of the first English colonies founded in North America. To formally found the colony, though, a charter was needed. In 1629, King Charles I granted the charter to the Massachusetts Bay Company, licensing the company to colonize and trade. It is more than likely that Charles did not realize this colony would harbor Puritan emigrants; rather, King Charles I intended to form an English-controlled company in the New World. However, in time, all business would be in the hands of the colonists.

Another wave of colonists soon settled in the same area. In 1630, a group of around 700 people in 11 ships came to the region. Due to the influx of colonists, new cities were founded. In September 1630, Boston was established, which would become one of the most important cities in colonial America due to the people who populated it and the ideas that emerged from there. Most of these early immigrants engaged in agriculture, while others were ordinary workers; these people represented around 95 percent of the population. The remaining 5 percent were shareholders, who ran the colony as well as church affairs. The founders of the colonies were men whose beliefs were contrary to the Church of England's teachings. These were the followers of the reform movement that erupted throughout Europe during the 17th century.

To fully understand the religious landscape, one must go back to the 16th century when there was general discontent in the Church of England. The pope's interference in church relations aroused great dissatisfaction among many inhabitants. The influence of Protestant philosophers and thinkers, who advocated living after the example of Jesus Christ, was beginning to permeate society. Also, a large number of people protested against the enrichment of the clergy. The selling of indulgences, which was a way to reduce the punishment for one's sins, enraged the people and brought even more dissatisfaction. Some reformists felt that separation from the Vatican was not enough and believed that the Church of England, the prominent religion in England, needed to be cleansed of all traces of Catholicism. This large group of like-minded people was called the Puritans.

One of the main notions of Puritanism was the theory of predestination, an outlook borrowed from Calvinism. This doctrine challenges the idea of free will by stating that one's destiny is decided upon birth. The Puritans also believed that all Protestant followers had a greater chance of salvation and that they would enjoy paradise in the afterlife. Puritan dogma did not require tolerance toward other religions. Puritan religious teachings indicated that all people were believed to be born innately evil and sinful, so it was necessary to live by strict beliefs to cleanse one's sinful nature and avoid eternal hell.

The early colonists in the Massachusetts Bay Colony mostly came from middle-class families in England. In most cases, complete families moved. Puritan families migrated to North America from every corner of England, yet most colonists came from eastern and southern England. A healthy environment and favorable living conditions were, in addition to the migrations, huge elements that resulted in population growth. Stable economic conditions led to more marriages and, subsequently, more offspring.

The initial stages of settlement of the New World brought many temptations and tribulations, so it was important to have strong leadership. In the Massachusetts Bay Colony, the idea of political organizing was first realized during the mid-1630s, leading to an elected assembly and a municipal court. The assembly consisted of representatives from each city of the colony, and voting was a luxury, as only adult men could vote. The governor and the representatives of the municipal court were elected every year.

One of the most prominent and politically significant characters of that time was John Winthrop. John Winthrop was born in Edwardstone, located in Suffolk, England, in 1588 into a well-to-do family. His grandfather was a wealthy man who made his fortune by producing textiles. Winthrop spent most of his youth working on a farm in Suffolk. He was a man of strict Puritan beliefs, striving to incorporate biblical practices into every segment of his life. Winthrop attended Trinity College for law, and by 1628, he had made much progress in his career, having obtained several important positions. Due to his religious beliefs, Winthrop lost more and more hope for his home country over time. Things worsened in England with Charles I coming to power in the 1620s. The Puritans were much closer to the English Parliament in terms of political activity. But the moment the king dissolved Parliament, a huge problem arose for the Puritans. The Puritans considered the king to be a dictator and sought to leave the country. As the situation became more and more complicated, the Puritans decided to leave England once and for all and head for the New World.

Before arriving in North America, Winthrop was appointed the governor of the Massachusetts Bay Colony by the Massachusetts Bay Company in 1629. He would land a few months later in June 1630, taking over the governorship from John Endecott. Winthrop had a natural gift for politics and management, and he successfully led the newly formed English colony. For Winthrop, going to North America was not an escape but a way to fulfill God's will and to "properly" organize the Church of England in a new territory. After becoming the governor, he organized several expeditions that brought Puritan migrants from England.

Winthrop pointed out to his people that their success lingered solely on mutual respect and appreciation. He loathed consumerism and pointed out that people should only spend what they needed and leave the rest for others. He encouraged gentleness, patience, and mutual understanding in the Puritan community.

Winthrop's mission was to essentially create a "perfect society." However, the first years in the New World were not easy. There was evident fatigue on the people's faces. Many decided to give up and return to England. Although the situation was exceptionally trying, Winthrop did not give up on his goal. He worked hard to prepare the colonists for the coming winter. Despite the hardships he faced, he never regretted his departure from England, which is evidenced by the letter he sent to his wife, Margaret, who had stayed behind along with the rest of his family. In the letter, Winthrop points out, "I thank God, I like so well to be here, as I do not repent my coming: and if I were to come again, I would not have altered my course, though I had foreseen all these Afflictions: I never fared better in my life, never slept better, never had more content of mind."

The first year brought extreme difficulties; the winter was long and harsh, and since the colonists arrived late, they failed to sow enough crops. As a result, food shortages were inevitable. Under such circumstances, there was a sharp jump in food prices. About 200 colonists died during the winter due to the difficult circumstances, and in the early spring, about 80 left the Massachusetts Bay Colony and returned home.

Once the winter was over, Winthrop sat down to work. His extensive education was of great importance for the formation of the colony's government. Various institutions were formed that were vital for the general organization of the newly formed colony. Winthrop surrounded himself with quality collaborators to sort out the situation as soon as possible. He was often able to calm tensions among the colonists by using his social skills, which allowed him to maintain harmony throughout the colony. John Winthrop was elected as the governor of the Massachusetts Bay Colony twelve times. He was fully committed to the colony's development until his death on March 26th, 1649.

The Massachusetts Bay Colony existed and operated as a joint-stock company; namely, the elections of authority figures operated on the principle that only men with sufficient capital or shares could elect other men to office. The name "Massachusetts" comes from the tribe who inhabited the area before the English arrived: the Massachusetts. This native tribe was almost extinct by the time the English permanently settled in the area. During the great pandemics of 1616 and 1619, the tribe was severely affected by infectious diseases. It is believed that the tribe initially had 4,000 members, and their numbers dwindled down to around 500 by the 1620s.

The settlements formed on the coast of New England had the potential to greatly expand, which was one of the reasons why massive migrations to this area took place. Rapid expansion was possible due to its favorable geographical position. The colonies of New England differed from others in the homogeneity of the population. Namely, in time, the area would be inhabited almost in full by only English. New England's population engaged in various activities, such as fishing, trade, and agriculture. Those who engaged in manufactory production were the most affluent stratum of society. The people produced everything, including food, clothes, shoes, and even furniture.

The river-rich area of New England was ideal for the development of trade. For centuries, the colony would be an unavoidable route for merchant ships. Since roads were almost nonexistent, trade mostly took place by the sea. The number of ships in New England continuously grew throughout the years, and the main raw material that was exploited was fish. Many of these ships were built by the fishermen themselves, and the Massachusetts Bay Colony became a very important shipyard over time.

In the colonies of New England, religion and education held a special place. The Puritans viewed the pastor as an intellectual and religious leader. The religious class was composed of willful and discerning leaders. These were the people who were "shod" by knowledge and contained all the characteristics that a true leader should possess. Crime and poverty in New England's colonies were a much rarer occurrence compared with other English colonies. This was the result of organized, capable leaders.

The fact that the life expectancy of the Puritans living in the New World eventually became significantly higher than that of their associates in England also speaks volumes about life quality. It must be noted that this took time; at the very beginning, the Puritans struggled to survive. One interesting phrase points out that the Puritans invented grandparents. Of course, they didn't invent grandparents, but given their longevity, many were fortunate enough to experience life with their children's children. Education and literacy rates in the colonies of New England were immensely high. Schooling was an obligation imposed by law, and every settlement that numbered over fifty people had to have a school financed directly from the tax system. Every Puritan wanted a child who knew how to read the Bible, which was one reason for the high literacy rate among the colonists.

In the end, the rise of the standard of living and the permeation of luxury into everyday life did not benefit the sophistication of the people, as strict religious rules still prevailed. Attending church sermons remained the obligation of every Puritan, and avoiding these obligations caused financial punishment. During church rites, a priest with a wooden stick patrolled the congregation. At one end hung feathers, which would tickle the chins of sleeping older men; at the other end was a wooden ball, which served as punishment for boys who laughed or were restless during the sermon.

It was previously pointed out that Winthrop worked intensively to settle the colony and form institutions to organize the new living space better. These institutions were imbued with religious elements, and in addition to the church and the governor, an important administrative body of the colony was created: the Court of Assistants. This institution was in charge of administering justice in the colony. The penal code in the colony was not clearly defined, so the people who held office made assessments as to how to mete out punishments. Bible guidelines were used in almost all court proceedings. In some cases, the intervention of clergy was required if the court had a more demanding case. At times, the population's dissatisfaction grew since all decision-making was in the hands of a few people. Over time, the colonists would receive written laws, which were still almost entirely imbued with religious elements. The code that was eventually drafted was called the "Body of Freedom," and it included about a hundred civil and criminal laws. The civil laws in New England's colonies were considerably more advanced than the laws in England. As for the penal laws, despite displaying more cruelty, they were more lenient than those in England. However, all legal regulations were based solely on the Bible.

The Puritans could not make wooden houses upon their arrival, so they inhabited dwellings that were covered with clay and moss with earthen floors. This form of housing construction was no innovation; rather, it was characteristic of Scandinavia and medieval Germany.

The only wooden dwellings in these early colonial settlements were buildings formed to protect against possible attacks by the Native Americans. Years after the first migrations, the first wooden homes would be built.

These homes would not have been ostentatious, as that went against their beliefs. This can also be seen in the clothing they wore. Leather was one of the basic materials from which clothing was made. Workers and servants dressed in garments that were mostly made of deerskin. Socks were made of various materials, and almost all shoes had exclusively wooden soles. Hats were both modern and popular, and leather gloves were an almost indispensable clothing article. As the population became richer and as imports and exports of goods in Boston stores increased, so did clothing made from various materials imported from England. The permeation of modern clothing among Puritan settlers led to a ban on silver, gold, and silk lace. These fashion standards imposed from the mother country were difficult to control. Thus, many colonists were taken to court for disobeying these laws. Lace, short sleeves, short socks, and clothing items that revealed body parts were strictly forbidden.

Unnecessary entertainment was forbidden in the Massachusetts Bay Colony, as everyone was supposed to focus on the community. Since Puritans were devoted to strict biblical rules, they made sure their children followed them, instructing them about the beliefs and rules they must follow to live a good life at a young age. Puritans followed the Bible almost literally. There were even cases of executions of children if the child hit a parent.

Puritan society was strictly patriarchal, which is most evident in their treatment of women and children. Women were allowed to attend religious ceremonies in the church, but they were forbidden to engage in politics, whether it was church- or government-related. Those who "deviated" from God's path were punished severely, and members of other religions were often hanged at Boston Common. Therefore, religious tolerance did not exist, and those Puritans who fled Europe due to religious persecution ironically endorsed these practices themselves. All those who strayed from the Puritans' religious dogmas were called nonconformists or dissidents, and the punishments were extremely brutal. Besides hanging, other forms of punishment were applied, such as flogging and imprisonment. For instance, adulterers in the community were severely punished, and they were often subjected to a public lynching. During the late 17th century, there were several trials of people accused of witchcraft. During this time, the Puritans condemned not only women but also men. Puritans often resorted to public lapidations of people accused of witchcraft.

Chapter 4 – The Events That Triggered the Pequot War

The Pequot tribe had strongly developed trade ties with the Dutch colonists, as the area around the Connecticut River (modern-day Thames River) was a central trading hub. Near the Pequot tribe lived their greatest rivals: the Narragansett tribe. The rivalry was present in various areas, but it was primarily a trade or economic rivalry. While the Dutch traded with various indigenous tribes, the Pequots claimed the right to trade relations with the Europeans, as they were the most powerful tribe in the area.

The Dutch, who began settling in North America in the 1610s, controlled the Hudson River, which was their most important stronghold. The most popular item for trade among the Dutch population was leather, primarily beaver, which was mainly used for making hats. On the other hand, the Pequots demanded metal objects from the Dutch, such as teapots, buckles, and hooks, which the Native Americans removed and sharpened as arrows. The Pequots also made amulets and different jewelry from these metal objects. The Native Americans, especially the Pequots, were an essential factor when it came to trade, laying the basis for the formidable economic war to come. The English believed that the Pequots were detrimental to trade, namely because the English sought to take the business into their own hands.

This attitude became more prevalent as the English began to colonize New England more intensively. But even before the establishment of colonies like the Massachusetts Bay Colony or the Colony of Connecticut, the English was in geopolitical competition with Spain. The famous British geographer Richard Hakluyt wrote as early as 1584 that settling in the Americas should be one of England's top priorities. He believed this was the only way to prevent the Spanish from settling the entire continent. And the English acted on this by first settling a colony on Roanoke Island, located off the coast of North Carolina, in 1585. Although this colony was not a success, the first permanent English colony, Jamestown, was soon established in 1607. After that, the English colonization of America intensified, and the number of English migrants grew steadily year after year.

King James I sought to intensify the English colonization of America. In 1606, the English Parliament founded the Plymouth Company to help settle America. In time, England would establish dominance over North America, while Spain directed its colonization efforts to South America. The establishment of English colonies meant a struggle for the commercial supremacy of North America. Soon, with its influence, the British colonial empire would completely oust the Dutch from New England. The number of British colonists grew so much over time that their actions began to threaten the main Dutch trade garrison called House of Hope or Fort Good Hope, which was built in 1633. Several houses were built next to the garrison, and two cannons were installed at the checkpoint, which provided additional security. A small number of soldiers stayed in the newly built trade facility, securing the checkpoint's goods. By doing this, the Dutch made their presence in the Connecticut area official.

Jacob van Curler, a representative of the Dutch West India Company, was in charge of obtaining the land for Fort Good Hope. He purchased it from the Sequins, a tribe that inhabited Connecticut.

Although the peaceful acquisition of land took place several times in North American history, the prevailing European belief was that the land belonged to them, not the natives, and oftentimes, the land was acquired through more violent methods. Also, when purchasing land, Europeans often used alcohol in negotiations to honor the Native Americans in an attempt to reduce the price of the land.

Part of this violence stemmed from the fact that the Europeans, especially the English, viewed the Native Americans as savages who needed to be civilized. The texts of Captains John Mason and Underhill, who were major players in the Pequot War, abound with derogatory labeling. Through the prism of religion, they call the Pequots barbarians and savages. John Underhill wrote about the Pequots before going to war, saying that God himself sought to punish the Pequots for their sins. Underhill often refers to religion in his texts and quotes biblical passages to justify the English colonists' actions. The Church itself supported colonization, emphasizing that every being should feel the "grace of Christ," i.e., be saved from hell.

As time went by, philosophers and thinkers criticized such beliefs, although it should be noted this kind of viewpoint was not prevalent among people at the time. Denis Diderot, who was active over a hundred years after the Pequot War, stands out as one of the men who advocated for better treatment of the natives. Diderot points out that Europeans were the ones who were uncivilized. He believed that culture imposes morality and strengthens the norms of respect. Yet, in the example of the European colonization of the Americas, Diderot states that these norms were not present because the individual was so far from their home country. The French philosopher further says that the American colonies became places of brutal clashes, primarily because the colonists were so far from their home countries and were not within the radius of firmly established organized, legal institutions. In this way, the habit of restraining one's instincts for violence was weakened.

However, in the beginning, the interactions between the colonists and the Native Americans were fairly peaceful. With the formation of the colonies in New England, the British came into contact with the Pequots and Narragansetts. The Narragansett tribe was the first of the two to enter into trade relations with the English. In 1632, they sent their envoys to the English, who expressed a desire to establish trade relations with their new neighbors, the Massachusetts Bay Colony. At first, the Pequots were not very interested in intensive cooperation with the English. In the same year (1632), they proposed to the Dutch that they set up new trading points on the Connecticut River to intensify their trade cooperation, primarily the "Good Hope" trade point. This proposal reached the prominent people of Plymouth Colony, who thought this move could potentially endanger their trade interests in the area. The English, therefore, sought to form their own trading post north of the Dutch one, thus devaluing the importance of the Dutch trading post. The leaders of Plymouth Colony presented their plan to the people living in the Massachusetts Bay Colony, as well as other smaller New England colonies. However, the first governor of the Massachusetts Bay Colony, John Winthrop, rejected the plan, pointing out that they did not want to interfere in these affairs. However, Winthrop lied when he said this, for he soon sent scouts to reconnoiter that territory, with John Oldham leading the mission. The reason Winthrop refused to cooperate was that he did not want to share the profits with others. After returning from his brief mission, Oldham brought great news to his governor, noting that it was a vibrant area and an excellent trading location. Plymouth, meanwhile, was forming its own trading base, ignoring the possible danger from the Dutch.

During this time, the Pequots continued their cooperation with the Dutch, but they were not the only tribe to do so. Other smaller tribes inhabited the same territory and also dealt with the European settlers. The Pequots considered them competition and, on one occasion, liquidated several members of a rival tribe after they ignored the warning of the Pequots to stop trading with the Dutch. The Dutch did not appreciate this act. Jacob Elkins, who ran Dutch trade in the New World, was furious since he had good trade relations with other tribal communities, and with this move, the Pequots threatened their trade with the Dutch.

In 1632, the Dutch captured the Pequot's sachem, Tatobem. As one might expect, these events completely halted trade between the Dutch and the Pequot tribe. For Tatobem's release, the Dutch demanded a large ransom, and the Pequots collected a large amount of wampum to pay it. However, after the Pequots paid the ransom, the Dutch killed Tatobem anyway. The Pequots were furious about this, saying that they would seek revenge for the murder.

The Pequots, intending to avenge their tribe, attacked a European merchant ship, killing crew members and the ship's captain, John Stone, on August 8th, 1634. However, John Stone was not Dutch but rather English. Stone was a merchant who traded goods from various parts of the world, including India, Britain, and the Americas. Yet, at that moment, no one really cared about his death. Stone's behavior had long damaged his reputation, for he led an extremely tumultuous life. Alcohol, blasphemy, and violence were the cornerstones of his life, to the point that the governors of the English colonies wanted no association with him. The Dutch even rejected Stone as a potential business partner. A few months before his death, Stone was accused of attempted piracy in Manhattan but managed to escape certain death. After that, Stone acted as a free trader.

There are several versions of what happened to Stone on that eventful day in August. The first version says that Stone sailed with a crew to a Native American village. After drinking alcohol, the crew became very violent, so the Native Americans killed them. Another version points out that the Pequots killed Stone by mistake, thinking that he was a Dutch colonist.

In the months that followed, serious problems began to rise up for the Pequots. Soon after, the Narragansett tribe declared war on the Pequots. Their sour relations were primarily due to the trade rivalry between the two tribes. The Mohegan tribe also joined the war alliance against the Pequots. Under such circumstances, the Pequots set out in search of allies.

At the time, the leader of the Pequot tribe was Sassacus, the son of the murdered tribal leader Tatobem. Sassacus decided to look for allies in the Massachusetts Bay Colony. In October 1634, he sent a delegation to the Massachusetts Bay Colony's headquarters to establish trade ties and friendship with the English. The English accepted this olive branch but only on the condition that Captain John Stone's killers were arrested so they could put them on trial. The Pequot envoys informed the English that Captain Stone's violent death was retribution for kidnapping several members of their tribe, as Stone had allegedly demanded that the prisoners be his guides on the Connecticut River. Another problem cropped up when the English leaders in Boston demanded more wampum than the Pequot had offered them. Some sources even state that the Puritans asked the Pequots to trade exclusively with them. The Pequot envoys informed the English that before the treaty was finalized, they wanted the English to meet with Sassacus. However, some sources say the Pequot envoys engaged in an oral agreement with the English, although there is no written evidence of this actually occurring. The only thing we can be sure of is that the English acted as peace mediators between the Narragansetts and Pequots, restoring peace for a short period of time. After this agreement, the English established three trading cities on the Connecticut River, which was one of the main trading points in the region.

Soon after these cities were built, the leader of the Mohegans informed the English that the Pequots intended to attack the newly formed English cities on the Connecticut River. The warning was taken seriously in Boston, the capital of the Massachusetts Bay

Colony. The English soon organized a new meeting with the Pequot envoys, repeating the same demands as before, with a particular emphasis on obtaining the assassins of Captain John Stone. The meeting did not go as expected, and the situation continued to spiral.

After the meeting, the English decided that the possibility of any negotiations with the Pequots no longer existed. Just days after the event, on July 20th, 1636, John Oldham, an important figure in the Massachusetts Bay Colony, was killed by Native Americans. What further infuriated the colonists was that John Oldham's body was found completely naked. They interpreted this act as an attack on Catholicism. English Captain John Mason wrote extensively on the events of the Pequot War. In his notes, he pointed out that the Pequots were a barbarian tribe and that this would not have been the first assassination of English colonists by them.

The English learned about the murder of John Oldham from Narragansett envoys. While the Narragansetts admitted that some of their men were involved in the murder, they claimed that the Pequots had organized the entire operation. The details provided by the Narragansett envoys were probably a lie, and to this day, no one is sure who should be held responsible for the death of Oldham. Most likely, Oldham was killed by members of the Narragansett tribe, as their age-old rivalry over trade with the Pequots, at times, targeted colonists who traded with the enemy.

The assassination of John Oldham was probably the tipping point. Although John Oldham had some disagreements with the authorities in the English colonies, he was a highly important community member. He played a significant role in trade, and the colonies of Plymouth and Massachusetts relied on his services. Oldham transported highly valuable goods, such as corn, which was one of the most important raw materials in the New World. He worked with the Native Americans as well, first coming into contact with them in around 1633. His death aroused concern among the colonists. Not only was Oldham their contact with other Englishmen in the area, but they believed this kind of brutality could happen to anyone—even their own families.

Although his murder is still largely a mystery, some accounts exist that help piece part of the puzzle together. John Gallop, a Boston merchant, discovered the boat in which John Oldham's body lay. As he approached Oldham's ship, Gallop saw a large number of Native Americans on the deck. At that moment, he hurried to get to the boat as soon as possible because he immediately suspected that something was wrong. When the Native Americans spotted him, they panicked and began to flee the ship. Several natives were caught and overpowered by Gallop's crew. A search of John Oldham's ship resulted in Gallop's crew finding the mutilated body of the unfortunate merchant. Gallop, highly infuriated and in fear of an impending rebellion on his own ship, tied some of the prisoners together and threw them overboard. Gallop first headed to Fort Saybrook to spread the news of the English merchant's death and immediately sailed to Boston afterward, where he submitted a detailed report on his colleague's death. The captured Narragansett said that members of the Narragansett tribe and their allies were behind Oldham's murder. John Winthrop concluded that Oldham had been killed because he found himself at the center of turmoil among the tribes.

There is another version of Oldham's death, in which the murder resulted from a transactional dispute between Oldham and the tribes with whom he collaborated. The third version, which was mentioned earlier and is the least plausible, was the one put forward by the Narragansetts, of how the Pequots killed Oldham. Winthrop also claimed that most of the evidence pointed to the natives living on Block Island. The small tribe that inhabited Block Island had close ties to the Narragansett and Eastern Niantic tribes.

There is much evidence to point to the guilt of the Narragansetts, yet the British chose to listen to their version of the events. Truthfully, the British could not afford to wage war against both the Pequots and the Narragansetts. Instead, they decided to wage war against the stronger tribe, the one that controlled larger territories and had more wealth. Also, the British had to take into consideration that the Pequots were responsible for the deaths of several members of rival tribes that traded with the Dutch, so the possibility that they may have been the culprit for the murdered merchant could not be completely ruled out. On top of this, the British still had a fairly fresh memory of the murder of John Stone. While Stone might not have been greatly loved by the community, his death could have been used as an additional impetus for war. Thus, the British colonists decided to launch a punitive expedition against the Pequots.

Although the English later made an alliance with other native tribes to fight against the Pequots, they at first targeted whoever they could get their hands on. The first move of the English was an expedition to Block Island. John Endecott was placed in charge of ninety men, and their goal was to punish the killers of John Oldham. Many of the soldiers led by Endecott (about 40 percent) were experienced fighters who had fought on European soil. Captain John Endecott himself is mentioned in historical sources as an experienced soldier with exceptional courage. He is said to have been an unyielding Puritan who showed intense intolerance of Roman Catholics.

John Underhill, an English captain in the Pequot War, made several reports of this event. His texts represent the most extensive material regarding the attack on Block Island, and he was also one of the commanders of that operation. Underhill points out that the effort to access the mainland of Block Island was initially impossible. After realizing the English were approaching the coast, the Native Americans showered the colonists with many arrows. Underhill also states that the Native Americans shot firearms, with some of the shots hitting the soldiers. A group of about fifty Manissean warriors offered violent resistance to the English, but their resistance was in vain. The English colonists soon reorganized, and the Native Americans began to flee. Most of the natives were able to flee, and the English, likewise, did not suffer much damage.

During this punitive expedition, the English set fire to several villages and cornfields on the island to send a strong message to the Native Americans. This action was a severe blow to the natives on the island, as the English destroyed large quantities of their food supplies and burned their crops.

The next stop of this punitive expedition was the territory under the control of the Pequots. The Pequots were oblivious to the English operations on Block Island, so they welcomed the English warmly from the shore. After the colonists did not respond to their greetings, the Pequots sent one of their elders by canoe to talk to the English. The demands of the colonists were exacting. Firstly, they once again insisted that the Pequots must hand over the assassins of Captain John Stone. The tribal leader who paddled out to speak with the English pointed out that the Pequots could not hand over Sassacus, noting that he had no choice and that he had to avenge his father's death. The tribal leader also expressed regret over the death of John Stone, reiterating once again that the Pequots thought he was a Dutch colonist and not an English one.

Underhill noted some more details during the negotiations between Endecott and the Pequot elder. He pointed out that the Pequots delayed the negotiations, which the English interpreted as a means to gain time for their warriors to organize. Also, it was noted that there were no women and children on the coast that day. Despite the warm welcome, this detail aroused suspicion among the Puritans, as the English interpreted this as a willingness to engage in military action. Also, Sassacus was not present that day; the tribal elder who spoke to the English colonists said that he had gone to visit one of the neighboring Pequot tribes. Endecott informed the elder that if the Pequots did not meet the conditions imposed from Boston, then the English would take twenty Pequot children as hostages. Such conditions would be difficult for any tribe to accept, especially the

Pequots. The tribe had been decimated by epidemics, and they could not agree to further reduce its population by giving the English hostages. Also, the English demanded some material compensation from the Pequots, as paying tribute to the English would create a subservient feeling among the Pequots, which would hopefully help guarantee their future good behavior. The Pequot elder was finally allowed to return to the coast and talk to the other members of the tribe about what the English had said.

In Underhill's account, the English became more and more impatient as time passed. Many believed the Pequots were readying themselves for war, as they could no longer be seen on the coast. Eventually, Endecott decided to attack first. The attack did not meet with significant resistance, and apart from the burning of homes and the looting of crops, nothing significant happened. Lion Gardiner, who was the captain of Fort Saybrook, and his men were the most active during this campaign, as there was a famine among his crew at Saybrook. Once the English dispersed, the colonists in the Connecticut area and at Fort Saybrook had to spend the winter alone, without support from Boston. In other words, they were left at the mercy of the enraged Pequot warriors. After this event, the Pequot War officially began.

Chapter 5 – Military Capacities, Organization, and Tactics of the Warring Parties

To better understand the course of the Pequot War, it is vital to get acquainted with the Puritans' and Pequots' military capabilities.

Pequot warriors had a lot of combat experience since they consistently fought with other tribes. These encounters involved a direct showdown on the battlefield, meaning there wasn't much use of tactics. The Pequots mainly relied on bows and arrows, with the occasional use of firearms. Some indicators show that the Pequots had dozens of rifles, but they seldom used them during the Pequot War. According to some information, the Pequots had slightly more than 1,500 warriors before the Pequot War broke out. This information is based on the number of warriors who died at the end of the war, which was around 1,500. It is logical to assume that not all the warriors were killed and that a small number of them managed to escape.

When the first battles with the English broke out, the Pequots had to completely change their approach to warfare because of the Europeans' armor and firearms. The Pequots were well aware of the fact that if they launched a massive attack, it would result in a complete catastrophe. So, the Pequots initially led small raids, which often ended fatally for the English. The natural surroundings and local environment allowed the natives to camouflage themselves more easily, allowing them to surprise the English. The Pequots also knew the disadvantages of European armor, and during the battles, they often aimed for the weak points, such as the neck, legs, head, or shoulders.

The structure of the attacks used by the Pequots in some situations is quite interesting. Namely, during the attack, several warriors fired arrows, after which they would throw themselves on the ground backward, thus leaving space for the archers behind to fire a new round of arrows. The arrows used back then had a range of about thirty meters (around ninety-eight feet). On the tips of the arrows, the Pequots placed sharpened bones, eagle claws, or metal heads made of brass. These metal tips posed the greatest threat to English soldiers, so the English sought to obstruct the Dutch trade with the natives early on, as this was one of the items that were often traded. Interestingly enough, the Pequots learned information about the European way of warfare from the Dutch, such as the importance of armor and the firearms they used.

The Pequots knew that the English needed time to reload their muskets, so they tried to use that period to attack. On average, a soldier took one minute to fire two shots, which meant about thirty seconds to reload. More experienced soldiers were able to fire up to three shots. An English soldier could easily hit a target in combat at a distance of between 50 and 75 meters (164 and 246 feet) in favorable conditions. During the fighting in the Pequot War, English troops mostly fired at the enemy from close distances. There are some indications that the Pequots asked English prisoners to show them how to make gunpowder, but this information is not entirely reliable.

The bow and arrow came to the forefront during the Pequot War. The Pequots tried to inflict damage on the English troops from a safe distance by firing from farther away. This was usually a distance of between 100 to 150 yards (between 91 and 137 meters). The Pequots used other weapons as well, including war clubs, tomahawks, hammers, axes, and knives, some of which were made of stone, bone, or iron. The use of European firearms was never fully utilized by the Pequots, which was to their disadvantage, as they posed a greater danger to the colonists. The main obstacle to the use of European weapons lies in the fact that the natives did not know how to service them, as they often broke down and were unreliable. The nature of Native American warfare before the Europeans' arrival also did not involve the use of heavy armor and protection, which the Europeans widely practiced.

Commanders, known as *pniese*, led larger groups of Pequot warriors. They were not sachems, but they were highly regarded in the community because of their knowledge and abilities. In 1623, Edward Winslow, who was the governor of Plymouth Colony three times, described his experience during an encounter with one of these *pniese*.

> The Pnieses are men of great courage and wisdom, and to these also the Devil appeareth more familiarly then to others, and as we conceive maketh covenant with them to preserve them from death, by wounds, with arrows, knives, hatchets...yet they are known by their courage and boldness, by reason whereof one of them will chase almost an hundred men; for they account it death for whomsoever stand in their way. These are highly esteemed of all sorts of people, and are of the Sachems Council, without whom they will not war or undertake any weighty business. In war their Sachems for their more safety go in the midst of them. They are commonly men of the greatest stature and strength, and such as will endure most hardness, and yet are more discreet, courteous, and

humane in their carriages than any amongst them scorning theft, lying, and the like base dealings, and stand as much upon their reputation as any men.

Also, among the Native Americans, there were cases of conflict resolution by two tribal fighters fighting each other. For that purpose, those warriors who were known as the best and the bravest in the tribe were chosen.

Such a situation was witnessed by English colonist Thomas Morton, who immigrated from Devon (England) to North America. Morton describes this struggle as follows:

> The two champions prepared for the fight, with their bows in hand, and a quiver full of arrows at their backs, they have entered into the field, the challenger and challenge-ed have chosen two trees, standing within a little distance of each other, they have cast lots for the chief of the trees, then either champion setting himself behind his tree, watches an advantage to let fly his shafts, and to gall his enemy. Then they continue shooting at each other, if by chance they espy any part open, they endeavour to gall the combatant in that part, and use much agility in the performance of the task they take in hand. Resolute they are in the execution of their vengeance, when once they have begunne, and will in no wise be daunted, or seem to shrink, though they doe catch a clip with an arrow, but fight it out in this manner till one or other be slaine.

As one can ascertain, the Pequots had one of the most respected military forces in the New England area. However, this partially led to their downfall in the war. The Pequots underestimated the European way of warfare, which meant observing the opposing forces, organizing troops, utilizing the appropriate tactics, and patiently waiting for the right moment to strike. These techniques were usual for European battlefields, which the English then transferred to North America.

Although this played a role in the outcome of the war, the main reason for the defeat of the Pequots was the technological supremacy of the Europeans, i.e., their use of muskets and armor. The musket first appeared in the 16th century, and it evolved over time. By the 17th century, the musket was the most used weapon. One would have to light a wick, which then lit the gunpowder and spat out a projectile. This projectile could be a round metal object or a stone. Muskets had a range of up to 140 meters (around 153 yards), but at a greater distance, they were useless. It was impossible to use muskets during the rain, and soldiers often experienced accidents due to the weapons malfunctioning. In any case, muskets were one of the factors that brought dominance to the English in the Pequot War.

Colonial soldiers were also armed with pistols, but this type of firearm was not very popular during military operations at the time. The reasons are multiple. These guns were used more often for close combat and not for military campaigns that required long-distance shooting. Also, the range of pistols during the 17th century was considerably less than that of the musket. A pistol could fire a projectile within a range of 35 meters (around 38 yards). The pistols were designed to insert two bullets at once, and when fired, both would be ejected. However, there is one similarity between pistols and rifles: the type of ammunition they used.

During the fighting at Mystic Fort, the use of firearms was not particularly stressed, as the settlement was densely populated. The fighting took place too quickly, and during the fighting, the English mostly used swords. The mandatory equipment of the European soldier during the 17th century included not only swords but also knives. Therefore, New England's colonial army had a wide range of weapons at its disposal. When we talk about armaments, it should be noted that English soldiers during the Pequot War used, to some extent, war axes, which were more characteristic of the arsenal of native warriors.

The colonists of New England sought to create a strong militia even before the Pequot War broke out. To this end, the English hired several experienced European soldiers, such as John Underhill, Daniel Patrick (a captain in the Massachusetts Bay Colony), and John Mason, who quickly adapted to the conditions in the New World. These were not the only experienced soldiers in the colonies, as a good chunk had taken part in the Thirty Years' War (1618–1648), a war that pitted the countries of central Europe against each other. These hired men intensively trained troops, showing them how to handle firearms and swords efficiently. They were well received into the Puritan community even though they were not members of their church. The Puritans accepted them as professionals who were there to do their job.

Another important factor contributing to the Pequots' defeat is that the English made a military alliance with the traditional enemies of the Pequots: the Narragansett and Mohegan tribes. In addition to gaining more men to fight in the war, the warriors of these tribes were also familiar with the terrain on which the battles took place and the military capabilities of the Pequots.

English colonists wore armored iron vests or heavy, long leather coats. At that time, this type of protection was excellent, and it allowed the English to significantly reduce the number of victims in their ranks. These coats were extremely expensive because the leather was of high quality and was produced in England. Hence, the colonists imported a large number of these coats as mandatory equipment for soldiers. The protection of soldiers also included helmets, which were of vital importance, and metal covers above the knees. And even though that kind of equipment was quite heavy and greatly restricted movement, it provided soldiers during the Pequot War with security. This equipment was produced throughout Europe; therefore, different models were available to the Puritans. John Underhill once pointed out that it was this protection that saved him from certain death.

The English tactics used during the war were reflected primarily during the Mystic campaign, which was the main campaign of the war. The troops were divided into two groups, which coordinated attacks, leaving the defenders with no chance of victory. The perimeter was encircled by assisting units that had a dual role. They "guarded the backs" of the majority of the troops, but they also captured all those who tried to escape from the fort. According to estimates from Mystic Fort, only a dozen Pequot survived, which speaks volumes about the efficiency of this type of organizing. The English tried to use the element of surprise several times during the Pequot War. These surprise attacks diminished the possibility for a quick and proper reaction by the Pequot warriors. It also prevented the Pequots from consolidating their troops, which gave the Europeans a better advantage since the Pequots had superior numbers.

During the Mystic campaign, the English worked intensively to gather intelligence, a technique unknown to the Pequots. For instance, John Mason constantly sent Native American scouts ahead of the bulk of English troops and their allies. These scouts consisted of warriors and guides of the Narragansett tribe, who updated Mason continuously about the situation that awaited him on the field. Mason was also given information about the Pequots' position by scouts who carried out daily activities during the advance of the English troops.

In addition to the tried and true tactics, the English also used newer techniques during the war with the Pequots, as they had to adapt to the Pequots' way of warfare. This was especially reflected during Endecott's punitive expedition to Block Island. On these occasions, the Puritans could not make full use of their military capabilities. They had to take longer breaks to attack at intervals, as their enemy was constantly on the move. Certainly, the experiences gained during Captain Endecott's expedition were later analyzed by the English and used against the enemy.

Chapter 6 – Conflict Escalation

The war came at an exceptionally trying time for both sides. The year before, the region had been hit by a hurricane, which devastated crops and demolished homes. The situation worsened because of the flooding, which took many lives and caused substantial material damage. As a result, the winter of 1635/36 was immensely harsh, and the lack of food led to the deaths of many animals, which subsequently caused another shortage of food for the people. The colony's distressing situation can be confirmed by a letter from a certain Edward Trelawny, who conveyed the events to his brother in England. "Currently, the country is in general poverty, a large number of people have arrived in the country." This period was also accompanied by the mass migration of English to North America, meaning there were more mouths to feed but not enough food to do so. Diseases also caused a demographic catastrophe among the local inhabitants, so there were not even enough people to cultivate the land. Another problem for the English was that they did not fully adapt to the North American sowing conditions. This new situation, according to some historians, hastened preparations for war.

The situation in the English fortress of Saybrook, where many actions of the Pequot War took place, was also complicated. Some sources point to the general dissatisfaction among the Saybrook inhabitants. Namely, the people residing in the fort wrote to the colony leaders about starvation and the shortage of clothes. The biggest problem the people faced was the lack of corn. This commodity was valued not only among the natives but also the European immigrants. Corn was easy to grow and fed both humans and livestock. It could also be consumed in many ways, such as dried, cooked, and baked in bread.

There was some dissatisfaction among the Puritans over the decision to go to war with the Pequots. Lion Gardiner, the commander of Fort Saybrook, pointed out that his crew was starving in a time of peace. He secretly hoped that the Native Americans would accept Boston's demands for fear of escalating the conflict. The crew at Saybrook had good reason to fear the oncoming war. Namely, the fortress was located near the Pequots, and there was the logical possibility that they would be the first to be attacked. However, over time, Gardiner changed his mind about the war because the opportunity arose for the English to gain the rich fields owned by the Pequots.

No matter what some of the Puritans might have thought or wished, a war was coming. The punitive expedition to Block Island, which was led by the experienced Captain John Endecott, was just an overture to the bloody war between the Puritans and the Pequots. However, the Block Island campaign itself did not result in significant human casualties on either side, although Endecott burned several villages and looted supplies.

After Endecott's campaign, the Pequots began looking for allies. They contacted the sachems of the Narragansetts and Mohegans, asking them to join in the war against the English. If the Pequots had gained this alliance, the war would have very likely turned out to be in their favor. First of all, they would have eliminated the enemy "from their doorstep," and the English would not have one but two powerful tribes against them. However, those tribes would decide later on to fight on the side of the English. In this way, any possibility of the

Native Americans joining together to war against the European immigrants was suspended. It seems that the long history of internecine conflicts between the Pequots and the Narragansetts was an insurmountable obstacle. Nevertheless, the Pequots were still an exceptionally vigorous opponent, with as many as twenty-six sachems of smaller tribes on their side. However, most of these alliances were not of great importance to the Pequots when the war began since most of the tribes remained neutral.

The Pequots were furious over the actions of the English; the burning of their villages and the destruction of crops aroused great disdain and hatred toward the European settlers. Lion Gardiner, who was in charge of Fort Saybrook, and Edward Winslow, the governor of Plymouth Colony, wrote to the leaders in Boston because of the reckless actions that had been organized there. These leaders pointed out that the problems had been solved, at least for a while. Therefore, Winthrop did not think that the Pequots would respond with military intervention. He considered the punitive expedition led by Endecott to be a warning to the Pequots, who he assumed would realize that they were facing a powerful enemy.

For the Boston leaders, this opinion turned out to be a mistake. At the beginning of 1637, the Pequots began planning more intensive military operations. They directed their first actions against the colonists living around the Connecticut River. Their guerilla-style attacks caused immense damage to the English. The beginning of 1637 was essentially revenge for Endecott's actions in the previous summer. During this period, around thirty English colonists lost their lives. Those who were captured alive by the Pequots suffered a worst fate: torture and a slow death.

There were occasional raids on Fort Saybrook, which was designed by Lion Gardiner and built at the mouth of the Connecticut River. In addition to its importance as a military base for the Puritans, it also had a large mill. The attacks on Fort Saybrook were intense, but the Pequots carried them out in smaller groups. Lion Gardiner provides some information about these events. "ONE DAY MEMBERS OF THE SAYBROOK CREW HAD TO LEAVE THE FORT TO PROCURE SUPPLIES. DURING NEGOTIATIONS WITH THE PEQUOT, THEY WERE ALLOWED TO PASS SAFELY THROUGH THEIR TERRITORIES. UPON OUR RETURN, OUR THREE MEN WERE AMBUSHED BY AN INDIAN. THE PEQUOT TRIBE'S WARRIORS ORGANIZED THE AMBUSH, AND ALL THREE WERE KILLED, AND THE GOODS INTENDED FOR THE CREW IN THE FORTRESS WERE LOOTED."

Soon, a conflict would take place that the English could not easily ignore. In April 1637, about 200 Pequot warriors attacked the small settlement of Wethersfield, which was stationed south of Hartford. On April 23rd, the Pequots carried out a sudden and fierce attack on the English colonists while they were carrying out spring planting. Among the Pequots' ranks were members of the Wangunk tribe. Six men and two women lost their lives in the Pequot attack. The Pequots and their allies also killed twenty cattle. The killing of these animals created additional problems for the colonists because it reduced their food supplies when there was already a food shortage going on.

In that swift raid, the Pequots captured two girls, who belonged, incidentally, to the richest man in Wethersfield. Sources state that the Pequots, as they canoed by Fort Saybrook, mocked the colonists living there. They showed them the bloody clothes of the slain colonists and ridiculed the captured girls. The two girls were eventually returned after a ransom was paid. Dutch traders mediated the exchange.

Many historians believe that this Pequot attack was an effort by the natives to destroy English supplies and create additional problems for them in an already difficult year. By doing this, the Pequots essentially told the English they were not welcome.

The events of April 23rd, 1637, made things irreversible. It can certainly be considered one of the turning points in the Pequot War. Instead of the surprise hit-and-run tactics, Sassacus and his tribe began openly showing aggression toward the Europeans. These actions served as an indicator of what was to come. A few days after the attack on Wethersfield, on May 1ˢᵗ, 1637, the Colony of Connecticut officially declared war on the Pequot tribe. The General Court in Hartford had no argument over this ruling; a war with the Pequots was the only option for the colonists.

Philip Vincent, a soldier at Saybrook, provides information about the actions of the Pequots in the area of the Connecticut River and their attacks on Fort Saybrook. His descriptions of the Pequot warriors are very captivating. He points out that they had an imposing physique and that they were extremely adept warriors. Vincent also describes the Pequot as a savage barbarian tribe that no one dared to go against in open battle. These descriptions help show why many of the other tribes feared the Pequots and how they posed a threat. According to Philip's testimonies, even many English soldiers were fearful of the Pequot warriors.

The actions of the Pequots around Fort Saybrook and the Connecticut River area lasted for months. In the early spring of 1637, the English officially made a war alliance with the Pequots' traditional enemies, the Narragansetts and the Mohegans. The English had learned of the Pequots' attempts to ally with these two tribes, and such knowledge was not at all pleasant to them, as a native alliance would have certainly crushed the colonists. This was just one of the reasons why the English were in a hurry to gather allies in this war. However, gaining native allies could, at times, be rather difficult. Some tribes distrusted the new settlers, and they didn't want to help the colonists only to be betrayed later on. In addition, the Puritans viewed the natives with some disdain.

During the Pequot War, an extremely bizarre practice took place, namely the exchange of body parts of a killed enemy. In occasional battles with the Pequots, the Mohegans and Narragansetts cut off body parts and wore them around their English allies, who, in turn, ridiculed their native allies. However, a similar practice was prevalent among the English settlers, as they often beheaded their enemies. The exchange of these war trophies was a form of strengthening the war alliance between them. This mechanism, that is, the gift between the different cultures and peoples of the time, displays a notion of authority. Anthropological observation of such phenomena indicates the flow of power.

The Puritans did not apply this process of desecrating a dead enemy's body; they only did it to prisoners of war. A large number of heinous offenders and thieves in Puritan society suffered a similar fate. In Puritan society, during the beheading process, the rest of the desecrated body was chopped up and divided into quarters. Persons convicted of high treason inevitably went through that kind of punishment. Throughout Puritan history, there have been cases where top government officials experienced such a fate.

In England, a person convicted of high treason would have their head decapitated in front of an audience, and the head would later be publicly displayed as a warning to others. The English would often boil the severed head to slow down the deterioration of the tissue. In this way, the heads remained "fresh" for days, which gave the impression that the head had recently been cut off, which, in itself, is a highly morbid act. The cheeks on the severed head were sometimes painted red, which gave an additional effect of freshness. This form of desecration of an enemy's body is present in the Puritans' religious texts. Since religion had an immense impact on every sphere of life, this phenomenon was frequent.

The Puritans justified their actions by religion. In the holy texts, King David launched a campaign to punish all the unbelievers of the world for creating a new Canaan. In a way, the Puritans identified with this act, as they sought to create a place in the New World that was purified of nonbelievers. It was with these elements of religion that the Puritans sought to silence critics after the Mystic River massacre, which will be covered in the next chapter.

However, the practice of profaning the body of a dead enemy was also present among many native tribes of North America. In addition to written sources proving this, there is material evidence of these practices. Namely, archaeologists have found bodies that lack limbs or skulls. Such customs were deeply rooted in many Native American communities. Warriors often carried home body parts of their slain opponents from battles. They then showed these body parts to their families, other members of the tribe, and tribal chiefs. In this way, they proved they had emerged victorious from the war. It also demonstrated a warrior's courage, as he had protected his community by putting his life on the line.

Many tribes practiced brutal torture, which was done in public. The captured warrior was expected to endure this physical torture bravely while being observed and scrutinized by his enemy. These bloody customs primarily involved cutting off the prisoner's hands or feet. The final act in this process was beheading or scalping the prisoner of war. Given that the Pequots often captured colonists alive during the Pequot War, it is safe to say that many of them suffered various forms of torture.

Many Native American tribes had an extremely peculiar view of such a public, bloody act. They believed that a captured warrior had a chance to redeem himself, as he had not died an honorable death on the battlefield but had rather fallen into the hands of his enemy. That is precisely why the tribes of North America expected courage from the warrior who went through these tortures.

Similar to the English, Narragansett warriors publicly hung the limbs of slain enemies, and they did the same with the Pequot warriors. During the Pequot War, Uncas and other warriors from the Mohegan tribe captured five Pequot men. After torturing them, they were decapitated, and the severed heads were taken to their Puritan allies. The severed heads were publicly exhibited in Fort Saybrook. In this way, Uncas strengthened his alliance with the European colonists. These actions were fairly common during the war.

The English often rewarded their allies during the Pequot War for bringing in body parts of the slain Pequots. After the Mystic River massacre, the practice of beheading and mutilating body parts of fugitive Pequot warriors continued. On one occasion, a sachem of a smaller tribal community visited Fort Saybrook to try to arrange a trade with the Puritans. Captain Lion Gardiner told him a trade was possible, but he had one condition. He asked the sachem to bring the severed heads of those Pequot who sought refuge in their tribe. All those who brought the limbs or heads of Pequot warriors were rewarded. This move allowed the neutral parties of the war to become more involved and assist the English.

The act of exchanging body parts, torturing, and beheading was not just characteristic of the Pequot War. Throughout history, similar examples can be found in many cultures and parts of the world. Today, in the 21st century, there are countries in which certain serious criminals and political dissidents are punished by cutting off body parts, desecrating a man after death, or being killed in public executions. For the most part, these are countries whose laws are based on totalitarian political principles and whose laws are derived from religious texts and beliefs. In other words, these are mostly societies that are not familiar with democratic principles and basic human rights and freedoms.

Chapter 7 – Mystic River Campaign

In the literature, the Mystic River campaign is also known as the "Mystic Massacre." We draw most of our knowledge about the largest and most massive military operation of the Pequot War from the notes of the direct protagonists of that event. Much of this information is provided to us by Captain John Mason. In addition to Mason, some information about the Mystic campaign is provided by John Underhill and Lion Gardiner. Historiography agrees on one thing; while all these sources can be considered reliable, they were all written by the victors of the Pequot War. Some oral history of this event survived, which was primarily transmitted by the Mystic River campaign participants and the small number of surviving Pequots, who then passed on their terrible experiences to future generations. In addition to these sources, historians can look at the archaeological evidence. Douglas D. Scott led several archaeological expeditions to learn more about the most significant battle of the Pequot War. Douglas Scott is considered to be one of the most renowned American archaeologists today. He has been awarded numerous recognitions by respectable institutions, such as the United States Department of the Interior, the National Park Service, and the Archaeological Institute of America.

The owners of plots in the neighborhood selflessly ceded certain sites so they could be surveyed, and metal detection clubs have, in some small part, also contributed to the research of the Mystic Fort site. Thanks to this research, today, we have a lot of data to utilize to better understand the Mystic River campaign.

The Puritan campaign in Mystic River represents the first major action in the Pequot War. Indigenous raids during the months-long siege of Saybrook allowed the English to gain some insight into the fighting capacities, habits, and movements of the Pequot warriors. The Mystic River campaign lasted from May 17th to May 27th, 1637. The campaign's culmination was the battle at Pequot Fort, better known as Mystic Fort (also spelled as Mistick Fort in some sources), which lasted over an hour.

The whole campaign was excellently organized by experienced English military personnel. The Puritans undertook extensive observation measures, mapped their approach, organized the men, and figured out how best to withdraw troops from the scene. Until the battle at Mystic River, all the other English military maneuvers, such as the action on Block Island, can only be viewed as punitive expeditions; the same goes for the Pequots, whose actions are often seen as raids.

The Mystic River campaign was primarily the result of the Pequots' attack on the colonial settlement of Wethersfield in late April 1637. A colonial court in Hartford indicted the Pequots for killing English colonists in the Connecticut River area and appointed Captain John Mason to lead future military actions in the war against the Pequots. In addition to the experienced Captain Mason, Robert Seeley, William Pratt, and Thomas Bull joined the operation. These three men served as lieutenants. Eight sergeants were also involved in the Mystic River campaign, and local authorities made their own contributions as well. They were ordered to procure twenty sets of armor, weapons for the soldiers, and other necessary equipment for the military operation. While local authorities were given detailed instructions on how much to procure, each soldier was required to bring one pound of gunpowder, four pounds of shot, and twenty bullets. The settlements that made the highest contribution to the Mystic River campaign were Hartford, Windsor, and Wethersfield. In addition to the allied Mohegan and Narragansett tribes, warriors from the Suckiaug (also spelled as Saukiog or Sickaog) tribe also joined the action.

The Puritans were resolute about sending troops seventeen days after they declared war, which speaks volumes about their determination to deal with the Pequots once and for all. The troops sailed from Hartford on May 10th, 1637, and the journey to their first destination took about seven days. The winds were blowing against them, so the journey took longer than anticipated. They finally arrived at their desired destination of Fort Saybrook on May 17th, 1637.

Mason received clear instructions from his superiors regarding the attack on the Pequots. After arriving at their destination, he met with Captain John Underhill and Lion Gardiner, with whom he discussed the plan of attack and other instructions dictated from the council in Hartford.

The original proposed route dictated from Hartford involved advancing along the Connecticut River and using the typical combat formations. But although this action relied on standard military formations and tactics, there was something novel about it: the support of allied Native American tribes. The English troops numbered about 77 men. The allied tribes contributed around 250 warriors, who were, for the most part, Mohegans and Narragansetts.

Underhill suggested they reject the original plan of attack. As it has already been pointed out, the Pequots had changed certain habits and approaches to war to better fight the English. Underhill knew this. In fact, Underhill understood the Pequots perhaps the best of the three campaign leaders because he had more experience with their war capabilities and resources. The plan presented by Captain Mason implied direct conflict, and Underhill knew the chances of such a skirmish were minimal or nonexistent. Since the Pequots knew the advantages of European armaments, it was almost certain that they would avoid a direct clash with the British.

There was another problem as well. The English were fighting on foreign ground. Although some men had lived there for a few years, their knowledge of the terrain paled greatly in comparison to the Native Americans. It helped the English to have some of the tribes on their side, but Underhill and Gardiner were skeptical of including them in their ranks. To many, the fact that the natives had recently been allies of the Pequots raised doubts. Gardiner wrote the following, "How they dared to trust the Mohegan Indians who themselves descended from the Pequot." There was an established opinion among the colonists that the natives were generally a volatile factor; such an attitude had been formed during the first years of colonization.

However, they had no better choice; native allies during the Mystic River campaign were necessary. Captain Mason understood this and spoke up in defense of the Native American allies. Mason recognized that the campaign could not succeed without people who possessed knowledge of the terrain. Also, the Mohegans and Narragansetts were able to provide information on the movements of the Pequot warriors and the deployment of enemy troops.

During the negotiations of the Mystic River campaign, Dutch merchants arrived at the fort. They returned with the two girls who had been kidnapped by the Pequot warriors during the attack on Wethersfield on April 23rd, 1637. Around that same time, the leaders of the campaign came to an agreement. The frontal attack that was supposed to be carried out along the Connecticut River was unanimously rejected. Instead, the Puritans decided to sail outside Connecticut territory to make the Pequots think their troops were leaving. Underhill's men joined the military operations, while Gardiner decided to ensure the surgeon at Saybrook provided medical assistance to the wounded soldiers.

On Thursday, May 18th, 1637, the expedition set out to attack fortified Pequot areas, with the first target being Mystic Fort. To get there, the English decided to go across Narragansett territory, as it was located near where the Pequots resided. The expedition arrived in the Narragansetts' territory on May 20th, but the troops had to wait a little longer for the attack, as bad weather occurred and the army's leaders had to meet with the sachem to discuss the plan of attack. The Narragansetts suggested that the best chance for success was to launch a surprise attack during the night. They also gave detailed information about the enemy's position and the locations they were about to attack. It was agreed that the Narragansetts would organize themselves outside the settlement and ambush those Pequots escaping from the attack. Miantonomi (also spelled as Miantonomoh), the sachem of the Narragansetts, offered the English their best guides.

In the end, it was decided that the English and their allies would continue through the territory of the Narragansetts, then through the enemy's territory until they reached Mystic Fort. The English commanders considered speed, secrecy, and efficiency to be the keys to the campaign's success, so any further delay was unacceptable. Time was of the essence, as any prolongation could lead to the possibility of detection.

Once the Mystic River campaign leaders concluded that the operation was already behind, they decided not to wait for reinforcements from the Massachusetts Bay Colony. On May 24th, the expedition embarked on a journey of thirty-five miles (fifty-six kilometers) and soon reached the Niantic fort. This fort was not one of the planned targets, but the English knew the Niantics were on fairly good terms with the Pequots. If the Niantics spotted the colonists' movements, they could then inform the Pequots, which would jeopardize the entire operation. Since they could not enter the fort, their only option was to surround it and prevent the Niantics from leaving.

Mystic Fort was around fifteen miles (about twenty-four kilometers) away from the Niantic fort. On the morning of May 25th, the bulk of Mason's troops continued their journey. During the day, the forces covered a huge distance, which took a great toll on their physical endurance.

Before the attack, Mason decided to hold a war council, where they once again went over all the details. This break allowed the soldiers to rest before the great clash with the enemy. The expedition soon learned that several other well-guarded strategic sites were in the immediate vicinity of Mystic Fort. However, at no point did such knowledge discourage Mason and his troops. Although the soldiers did not have enough time to rest from their long journey, it was decided they would attack the fort. Before the attack, the Puritans joined in prayer, which was something they typically did before an immediate battle.

The English counted on the surprise factor. The ideal scenario would be to catch the Pequots asleep. It is not known when exactly the English attacked, as the sources differ. According to some information, the attack started one hour after midnight, while other sources state the English attacked four hours after midnight.

The troops were divided into two groups, with one led by Captain John Mason and the other by John Underhill. The plan was devised in this order: Mason would attack from the east entrance, while Underhill led the attack from the west. Tall wooden pillars surrounded the fort, and the entrances were camouflaged, yet that didn't prevent the guides from discerning the paths to the entrances. Mystic Fort covered about two acres of land, and the attack was supposed to be coordinated so that both groups attacked simultaneously.

However, things rarely go as planned. As the English approached the fort, dogs began to bark, revealing the presence of the English soldiers. One member of the Pequot tribe saw the English and began to alarm the others. At that moment, the English decided to attack, even though the troops were not in the agreed positions.

Mason's force met with fierce resistance from the natives, especially when he entered the settlement, for the fighting had intensified. The interior of the fort was densely populated. Mason's group suffered some losses but continued to suppress the Pequots. The Pequots, who had many of their best warriors in the fort, fought bravely. It is believed between 100 and 150 Pequot warriors were inside the fort. Testimonies say it took five soldiers to defeat just one Pequot warrior. At one point, Mason realized that if the fight continued at that pace, the operation could end unsuccessfully, as it would be too difficult to eliminate all the natives in the fort with the number of soldiers he had left. There were also many wounded among the English ranks, which made Mason's position even harder.

Due to these circumstances, Mason was forced to rethink his strategy. He decided to set fire to a dwelling inside the fort, and his soldiers followed his example. John Underhill describes the details of Mason's move as such:

> Captaine Mason and my selfe losing each of us a man, and had neere twentie wounded: most couragiously these Pequeats behaved themselves: but seeing the Fort was to hotte for us, wee devised a way how wee might save our selves and prejudice them, Captaine Mason entering into a Wigwam, brought out a fire-brand, after hee had wounded many in the house, then hee set fire on the Westside where he entred, my selfe set fire on the South end with a traine of Powder, the fires of both meeting in the center of the Fort blazed most terribly, and burnt all in the space of halfe an houre; many couragious fellowes were unwilling to come out, and fought most desperately through the Palisadoes.

This move is considered to be one of the main actions that led to the success of the Mystic River campaign. There are certain indications that the English would have failed if Mason had not decided to utilize fire. As one will shortly see, the Pequot War is characterized by unconventional military maneuvers, which further reflects the brutality of that short-lived but bloody war.

When the fire broke out, Underhill and his troops attacked immediately, demonstrating his experience and quick wit in battle since none of this had been planned. Underhill's men entered the fort armed with firearms and swords. The northern part of the fort was already on fire, and Underhill and his men followed the example of Mason and continued to set fires. When Underhill noticed Mason's troops had advanced, he decided to withdraw his contingent to outside the southwest entrance to the fort and continue fighting there.

Many Pequots tried to escape the fortress, especially in moments when the intensity of the English attack was too great. Thankfully, for the English (and unfortunately for the Pequots), one thing went according to plan. Several troops, mostly composed of native warriors, had surrounded the fort to prevent the escape of the Pequots. Thus, most of the people who managed to escape from Mystic Fort fell into the hands of the Mohegans, Narragansetts, and Suckiaugs and were killed. Sources indicate that the warriors of the Pequot tribe fought bravely to their last breath.

The end of the battle showed all the destruction and devastation that had been wrought. Sources differ, but between 400 and 700 members of the Pequot tribe lay dead in or near Mystic Fort. Most sources indicate that a little more than 400 people lived in the fort before the attack, and since almost everyone lost their lives that day, the estimate of a little over 400 people is the most likely. The largest number of casualties were women and children. It is estimated that the majority of the victims died in the fires caused by the English. The English casualties, on the other hand, were incomparably smaller. Two soldiers were killed, while a large number were wounded. Over 30 percent of the Puritan soldiers were seriously or lightly wounded in this battle, which lasted for over an hour. The native allies also suffered casualties; however, the exact number of how many died or were wounded is not known. Many of them suffered at the hands of the English themselves since they could not distinguish their native partners from the Pequots. As a result, the English shot their allies.

The returning journey posed an even greater challenge to the English and their Native American allies than the battle at Mystic Fort, as they had to carry a large number of wounded soldiers through enemy territory. Immediately after the battle, a temporary military camp was formed since they expected a Pequot counterattack. Hundreds of Pequot warriors from neighboring villages gathered on the nearby hills. Fear reigned among the English and their allies, but they didn't have much time to dwell on it, for the Pequot response was so quick that the English had no real time to rest. The Pequots kept out of reach of English firearms, so Underhill sought to mobilize the Mohegan and Narragansett warriors to form a defensive formation, which managed to repel the Pequots.

Some warriors of the Narragansett tribe feared that the English would run out of ammunition and decided to leave the campaign and return to their territory. This move shows how the allied tribes relied on the English and their technological military achievements. About fifty Narragansett warriors decided to leave the campaign. On their return home, they were attacked by the Pequots. However, Underhill decided to help the allies, jumping to their assistance with about thirty soldiers and saving the runaway Narragansetts from certain death. At that moment, the rest of the English troops were endangered, considering that Mason was left with a large number of wounded and without the thirty soldiers that Underhill took with him.

The Pequots were unsuccessful in their first two attempts to attack the English and their allies, and to make matters worse, they lost even more warriors. The counterattack lasted about an hour. The English decided to retreat to the designated point, the Thames River Harbor, which was accompanied by a series of counterattacks by the Pequot warriors. Mason states that about 300 warriors participated in the largest Pequot counterattack. Most of these counterattacks were successfully repulsed, which inflicted heavy losses on the Pequots.

Mason and Underhill formed a column with their wounded and descended Pequot Hill from the west slope. Mason led and guarded the wounded column with his soldiers, while Underhill was at the back of the column with his units. About 100 Pequots attacked the back of Underhill's column. A large number of them directly attacked the English, so they were easy targets for muskets. Part of that group attacked from the sides but without success.

The return journey was exceptionally trying and exhausting, and danger lurked constantly. Since the Pequots were trying to attack from all sides, protecting the wounded from the front and rear was not enough, so the English reinforced the sides as well. Most of the Pequot counterattacks were carried out from nearby swamps, and the English soldiers would occasionally open fire preventively in the direction of the swamps they encountered.

The attacks continued until the column was about two miles (just over three kilometers) from Thames Harbor. Sources indicate that the Pequot lost more warriors in these counterattacks than in the battle for Mystic Fort. This information is reported to us by Underhill, who talks about the Native Americans' disorganization in the military sense. To get revenge on the English as soon as possible, the Pequots had pushed forward without a concrete plan of attack, inflicting much damage on themselves in the process.

Underhill continued to advance toward the ships with the wounded and soon sailed for Saybrook. In the meantime, Mason continued to march to the east coast of Connecticut with the remaining troops on May 27th, 1637. Mason's troops encamped for another night, and early in the morning, they set out for Saybrook. There are certain indications that Sassacus tried to retaliate with fifty warriors, but this information must be taken with a grain of salt since it is not completely reliable.

On June 2nd, 1637, the General Court provided Mason with another thirty men to continue his fight against the surviving Pequots. Sassacus found himself on the run with about 200 members of the tribe, which included both warriors and civilians. Several military units were organized in the Connecticut area to hunt down the runaway Pequots. Some of the soldiers even came from the Massachusetts Bay Colony. In the meantime, Plymouth Colony declared war on the Pequots. The hunting and killing of the Pequot tribe that had managed to survive continued for a week after the Mystic River campaign.

In the area around Fort Saybrook, no attacks were carried out by natives, attacks that had been occurring almost every day, which speaks volumes about the devastation in which the tribe found itself. The Mystic River campaign inflicted incalculable damage on the Pequots, and every attempt to recover was unsuccessful. Some sources indicate that the allied tribes of the English, who, as we saw above, were an extremely important factor in the battle, agreed to cooperate with the Puritans on the condition that women and children be spared. If this actually took place, the Puritans most certainly ignored this deal since most of the victims in Mystic Fort were women and children.

The members of the Pequot tribe from nearby areas who came to Mystic Fort after the English departed were appalled by the sight; they had not seen anything like it before, nor was it clear to them how men could carry out such an atrocity. Even some English soldiers were disgusted by the scale of the massacre that had ensued in Mystic Fort. Still, Underhill pointed out that it was God's wrath against the ungodly savages, which was a belief most Puritans held.

The killing of the fleeing natives continued almost daily. Sources from that time indicate that some colonial cities, such as Hartford, were flooded with the limbs and heads of runaway Pequots, which, as mentioned above, were often brought in by other natives, whom the

English then paid. This practice lasted for weeks after the Mystic massacre.

The end of the Mystic River campaign also led to the enslavement of a large number of Pequots. Most of them were sold to colonies outside of the New England area so that they could not easily return to the territory that their ancestors had inhabited for hundreds of years. A large number of women and children were sent to live with the English allies. These unfortunate women and children typically ended up as servants in the Narragansett and Mohegan tribes.

As one can tell, after the Mystic River campaign, the Pequot tribe, which had once been mighty and strong, was put into the unfortunate position to fight for its survival overnight. There are certain indications that Sassacus and his surviving warriors sought to attack the English; however, he did not have enough men to carry out that plan. The survivors eventually set fire to their settlement out of helplessness and eliminated all the Mohegans in their ranks. Sassacus fled the Connecticut region, as he and his members were wanted by the English. He found temporary refuge with the Mohawk tribe.

The Mohawk tribe soon learned through merchants' stories of the extent of the brutal English attack on Mystic Fort. Fearful of the English attacking for providing refuge to the Pequots, the Mohawks liquidated Sassacus and all those who came with him. His head was first sent to Hartford, and by August, it was in Boston.

The last battle between the English and the Pequots took place between July 13th and 14th,1637. It was a shorter episode known as the Fairfield Swamp Fight or as the Great Swamp Fight. After the Mystic massacre, a group of Pequots escaped to what is today Fairfield, Connecticut, where the Sasqua tribe lived. In that skirmish, there were members of the Sasqua tribe, besides a few dozen Pequot warriors.

Around 160 soldiers from the Massachusetts Bay Colony managed to locate the Pequots, who were hiding in a swamp near modern-day Fairfield, Connecticut. The English surrounded them, preventing any attempt to escape. According to English estimates, there were between seventy and eighty warriors and several children and women inside the circle made by the Puritans. The children and women were taken as prisoners, while the tribe's warriors offered their last resistance to the superior Englishmen.

Initially, there was a constant fire of English muskets and Native American arrows. Sources point out that the Pequots also owned several firearms by this time. After the English consolidated the ranks, secured the circle, and made sure that the enemy had nowhere to run, on the foggy morning of July 14th, a proper attack was carried out.

The last resistance of the Pequots was broken. It is believed all the Pequot warriors who fought in the Great Swamp Fight died. The British suffered no casualties, but there were several wounded soldiers. This military operation and the assassination of Sassacus ended the Pequot War.

The Treaty of Hartford between the English and the tribal leaders of the Mohegan and Narragansett tribes was finalized on September 21st, 1638, officially ending the Pequot War, although the fighting had pretty much ended over a year ago. The territory previously controlled by the Pequots came into the hands of the English. The allied tribes that had participated in the war received a large number of Pequots as slaves. In return, they had to declare loyalty to the English.

By 1638, the subjugation of the survivors and the elimination of the Pequot tribe was complete. The trade that had previously been in the hands of the Pequots in the Connecticut territory fell into the hand of the English. The Treaty of Hartford banned the tribal name of "Pequot." From that point forward, any Pequot would be referred to as either a Mohegan or a Narragansett. Thus, the Pequot tribe was almost wiped off the face of the earth.

It can be easy to judge the English for what they did based on our modern understanding of right and wrong. The Mystic River campaign and the terms in the Treaty of Hartford would be entirely unacceptable in this day and age. However, back then, this kind of warfare was typical. While the Native Americans in New England engaged in massacres, which rarely included the killing of women and children, although it most certainly happened, they were not used to this scale of brutality, but many of the colonists were more than familiar with it back in the Old World. What drove the English in the Pequot War was not the thirst for blood but rather the thirst for victory. And to achieve such a victory, the leaders of the colonists used tactics that had already been established in Europe. The conflicts in England, the wars with other European countries, and the wars in Ireland show the same intensity of violence demonstrated during the Pequot War and other wars with the natives of North America.

And in addition to the many experienced soldiers who took part in the war, there were also many recruits who had a strong desire to prove themselves in battle and eventually advance in military service. They believed that by following their leader's orders and winning a decisive victory against their foe, they were on the best path to making a name for themselves in the New World.

Religion also played a major role in the decimation of the Pequots. To the English, war was much more than killing enemies; it was understood as a struggle for higher, divine goals. This was not a new concept to them either, as it had been deeply rooted in European society for many, many years. The involvement of the Church made things even more complicated, as violence became the subject of propaganda of the state and the Church. Soldiers who fought in wars believed their engagement was derived from a higher purpose; it was not just a mission to defend their state and family, nor was it a way to gain fame, material rewards, or decorations from rulers.

The English saw this fight as a matter of life and death. They were new to this land, and being overrun by the natives, who they considered to be inferior, would not only be insulting but would result in their own demise. If the English won, not only would they prove themselves to all the Native Americans, but they would also gain the wealth the Pequots had, allowing the English to prosper.

The Native Americans, on the other hand, had no religion-based goals to achieve during the Pequot War. Their understanding of the spiritual world had a completely different outlook from the European one. And the Pequots also did not fight for economic or political reasons. Although the natives were more than accustomed to warring with other tribes, many of the tribes in the New England area lived fairly peacefully together. At the same time, though, their battles could be incredibly brutal and bloody. However, Native American war practice in New England did not involve the mass killing of women and children of an enemy tribe. Very rarely were women and children killed by the New England tribes, and it definitely never happened on such a massive scale before the attack on Mystic Fort. For the most part, the New England tribes generally took prisoners. In this way, they sought to increase their numbers and compensate for any losses during the war.

Chapter 8 – The Mother of All Crimes

The Convention on the Prevention and Punishment of the Crime of Genocide was the international legal instrument that codified the crime of genocide for the first time. It was adopted by the United Nations on December 9th, 1948. The Convention defines genocide as the intent to destroy a national, ethnic, racial, or religious group in whole or in part. Genocidal acts include killing members of a group, violating the group members' physical or mental integrity, deliberately subjecting group members to living conditions that could lead to the complete destruction of the group, measures to prevent the group's birth rate, and forcible relocation and deportation. This is why genocide is known as the "crime of all crimes" or as the "mother of all crimes." However, the definition of genocide itself is problematic for doctrinal and material reasons and often arises from disagreements and controversy to prove genocidal acts.

This short overture on the character and definition of genocide is important to understand. Modern historians are conflicted as to what happened in the Pequot War, particularly during the Mystic massacre. Some believe the aggression of the English was justified, while others believe it was more akin to genocide. It is important to consider both views so one can gain a fuller understanding of what is being discussed in the academic community. In this chapter, we will look at the possible genocidal acts of the Pequot War, examine other factors, and present the thesis and antithesis of the "mother of all crimes" in North America.

One of the most common definitions of genocide in use is the one given by Polish lawyer Raphael Lemkin, who was of Jewish descent.

> Generally speaking, genocide does not necessarily mean the immediate destruction of a nation, except when accomplished by mass killings of all members of a nation. It is intended rather to signify a coordinated plan of different actions aiming at the destruction of essential foundations of the life of national groups, with the aim of annihilating the groups themselves. The objectives of such a plan would be the disintegration of the political and social institutions, of culture, language, national feelings, religion, and the economic existence of national groups, and the destruction of the personal security, liberty, health, dignity, and even the lives of the individuals belonging to such groups.

As we will have the opportunity to see in this chapter, the Mystic River campaign depicted many elements of Lemkin's definition. This definition is used by many scholars to prove genocidal acts took place in North America. Raphael Lemkin's definition of genocide was also adopted through a United Nations resolution.

Genocide, as a legal norm, is relatively "young." However, its practice has been in use since the dawn of the first civilizations. Mass torture and deaths were not only unique of the Second World War. Still, the scale of suffering in that war was so massive that the United Nations legally passed a convention on genocide at the international level. The resolution was also passed to prevent future mass casualties, as well as to prevent wars. Violations of basic human rights have been reflected throughout all historical epochs and are characteristic in almost all world cultures. As a legal term, genocide is mostly the subject of law, but genocide is also present in historiography, political science, anthropology, sociology, and philosophy. It can also be observed from a psychological point of view.

In the context of the international law passed in 1948, the campaign on Mystic Fort had elements of genocide. The Puritans' actions in what was essentially the final phase of the Pequot War were aimed at the systematic destruction of an entire tribe. The actions at Mystic Fort included killing civilians and forcibly deporting the survivors with the purpose of exterminating an entire group. The Europeans gave themselves the exclusive right to sovereignty in the New World and extinguished all elements of the Pequots' autochthony.

Proponents of genocidal action against the natives point out that the Pequot War's biggest battle was just an overture to what followed decades after the war. In the years after the Pequot War, the natives of North America experienced a demographic collapse, with some tribes being completely exterminated.

Some sources indicate that the Europeans deliberately transmitted infectious diseases to the Native Americans through the trade of blankets. However, there is no real evidence to point to a systematic plan to infect the Native Americans with disease. However, proponents of the thesis of genocidal actions have a stronger argument when it comes to population demographics. Through the decades of European domination of North America, the number of native peoples was brutally reduced. Over time, the Europeans viewed the people who had lived in the country centuries before they came as a hindrance.

Certain high-ranking people in politics indicate the extent of the indifference toward Native American tribes during colonization. The first governor of California, Peter Burnett, called for a war of extermination against the Native Americans, one that would continue "until the Indian race became extinct." Burnett called for this war because he believed that Native American tribes were preventing expansion and progress in the exploration of mineral resources in the area of California. In the following period, the authorities eliminated thousands of members of the Yuki tribe, who had inhabited the northern parts of California. Like the Pequots, there are not many members of the Yuki tribe left today. Unlike the Pequots, the Yuki might never be able to recover their language.

Later on, many Native American children were forced to attend boarding schools, where they were taught lessons in English and learned English customs, which helped contribute to the demise of their own languages and traditions.

These events have a distant echo that one can still hear today. In the modern era, there is still a certain amount of prejudice against Native Americans. Such an attitude toward the natives results from centuries of unfounded stigmatization of the indigenous peoples of North America.

However, it is important to examine why historians believe what took place was not genocide. Many scholars state that the Europeans' attitudes toward Native Americans can be defined as a crime but not genocide. To defend their thesis, they look at the vague figures of Native American demographics that anthropologists have presented to the public. And indeed, so far, scientists have not come close to agreeing on an exact figure or even an approximate figure. In the 1920s, it was reported that about 1.5 million Native Americans lived in America during the arrival of the Europeans. In 1987, it was believed that the figure was about 5 million natives. Finally, it was stated that before the arrival of the Europeans, the number of Native Americans was 18 million people.

While no one can argue that many Native Americans died in wars with the Europeans, many also died in battles with each other, as the natives did not always get along. Also, as mentioned above, an incredibly high number of Native Americans suffered and died from various diseases. Smallpox caused the most damage, for this disease did not discriminate based on age. Therefore, many adults fell ill, so there was no one left to fully cultivate the land and to hunt. Thus, many tribes died of starvation.

Considering that "intent" is one of the key elements of the definition of genocide, many scholars think that the Europeans who transmitted infectious diseases to the natives had no intention of doing this. There were some occasions where the Europeans deliberately contaminated blankets, but those are isolated cases and not a common practice; therefore, it did not represent the official attitude of the colonial governments.

As one might expect, the crime perpetrated against the Pequots, whether it was genocide or not, contains elements of racial and religious intolerance toward the natives. The Puritans lived according to their religious beliefs, which were deeply ingrained in their everyday life. They believed that Jesus Christ was sent to Earth to save several people or the "chosen ones." Their dogmatic beliefs implied rigid adherence to certain rules; they valued cleanliness and were wary of the forest, as the forest was, according to their beliefs, Satan's home. The natives were deeply connected with the forest and nature, which was incomprehensible to the English. The sources that are generally used to reconstruct the Pequot War are flooded with elements of religious intolerance. Underhill, Mason, Gardiner, and Winthrop all characterize the Pequots as atheists, savages, and Satan's servants who need to be destroyed. To this end, after the Mystic River campaign, John Mason wrote the following:

> Let the whole Earth be filled with his Glory! Thus the Lord was pleased to smite our Enemies in the hinder Parts, and to give us their Land for an Inheritance: Who remembred us in our low Estate, and redeemed us out of our Enemies Hands: Let us therefore praise the Lord for his Goodness and his wonderful Works to the Children of Men!

These elements of religious extremism were directed at all the Native American tribes of North America equally.

Elements of racism were the product of several different factors. Religious persecution, the birth of a national identity, and geographical discoveries are all factors that led to the formation of racial intolerance. And although some of these factors brought about progress and a shift in humanity, such as geographical discoveries, racism emerged as a negative result. The initial contacts between the European immigrants and the Native Americans did not allude to open racial intolerance, but as their contact intensified over time, racial discrimination against the natives became more pronounced. Eventually, the natives were seen as racially and politically inferior in the Europeans' eyes. Contributions to science and technology and the birth of a national entity laid the fertile ground in which racism could blossom.

The development of a national identity meant the people shared a common language and culture, as well as racial and religious unity. While this brought together one group of people, it created intolerance toward others. When we talk about the development of science and its impact on the emergence of racism, one can look at the advancements in biology. During the early stages of the Enlightenment, which began in 1715, the classification of flora and fauna took place. This classification would eventually be raised up as an example of one group's racial inferiority over another. Developments in technology brought about practices that one can equate with capitalism. For businesses to perform at the highest level, the enslavement of certain peoples for economic gain became a common practice.

However, the first stage of English colonization of the New World was conceived in a completely different way, as the English believed they would bring justice and religious enlightenment to the Native Americans. Since the Spaniards were ruthless toward the natives, the English tried to prove that they were superior to the Spaniards. These initial efforts soon turned into the struggle for supremacy over North America.

Chapter 9 – Analysis and Comparison of King Philip's War and the Historiography of the Pequot War

The Pequot War was the first conflict in New England between the Native Americans and the European colonists, and it permanently changed the relations between the Europeans and Native Americans. The balance of power changed quickly, and the numerous but disorganized natives of North America came to be subordinate to the Europeans. By destroying one of the most powerful Native American tribes in New England, one obstacle to the Puritans' intensive spread on North American soil was removed.

After the war, British authorities established complete domination over the economy and trade in that part of North America, as the Pequots were no longer able to provide a buffer to their expansion. In the years after the Pequot War, that area of North America was intertwined with global economic trends, as the Puritans involved the New World in the European mercantilist system. A more intensive penetration of capitalist ideas began to flow into North America.

Some tribes adopted these economic patterns, and even the monopoly over wampum came into the hands of the English.

The Pequot War showed the English settlers' determination for territorial expansion at all costs. In the 1630s, there was a mass migration of Puritans to North America. Statistics show that the end of the Pequot War significantly increased the influx of new people to New England. Thus, one can conclude that the colonists' victory in the war influenced the mass migration of Puritans to the New World since all obstacles to English domination had been removed.

After the Pequot War, the Native Americans and Puritans lived in relative peace. While there was the occasional raid, for the most part, things had settled. This all stopped when King Philip's War broke out in 1675. Many historians consider King Philip's War to be the continuation of the Pequot War, as it was necessary to "jump over" another barrier to expand English influence. While the English pursued economic interests during the Pequot War, King Philip's War was a battle for territory. After the Pequot War, the Puritans saw all tribal communities as subjects who had to abide by the colonies' instructions and imposed laws. It was extremely difficult for the natives to submit to the colonists' laws, as they opposed their traditional patterns, notions, and belief system.

When we talk about the causes that led to King Philip's War, most historians agree that the main factor was the usurpation of tribal land by the Puritans. The mass migration of English settlers to the New World had created the need for expansion, which came at the expense of the native tribes. The English tried to take over the natives' land, which eventually resulted in a bloody war.

The name of the conflict is related to the name of the sachem of the Pokanoket and the grand sachem of the Wampanoag Confederacy, Metacomet, who took the English name of Philip to become more closely tied to the English. Metacomet sought an alliance with Plymouth Colony, and although they entered into an agreement, he soon realized they wouldn't help the tribe as much as they had promised.

In late January 1675, a corpse of a Native American was found in a pond in southeastern Massachusetts. However, this wasn't just any ordinary person. This man was John Sassamon, and he was what was known as a praying Indian. These were Native Americans who had converted either willingly or unwillingly to Christianity. It is estimated that over 1,600 Native Americans in the Massachusetts Bay Colony and Plymouth Colony had accepted Christianity prior to the war. It seems that Sassamon, who was from the Massachusett tribe, was a willing convert, as he spread Christianity to nearby tribes. Sassamon was also of import to the English because he could read and write in English and also served as an interpreter. Before his death, he warned the English that Metacomet was planning an attack. Initially, when the Puritans found Sassamon's body, they thought he had an accident. But upon closer inspection, they realized his neck was broken. Many thought that John Sassamon had been killed under the sachem's order, who was seeking vengeance on John for adopting English customs and religion. It is also possible that Metacomet found out that John had revealed his plans. In June, three Wampanoags were tried by a jury on suspicion of participating in the murder of the baptized John Sassamon. Interestingly enough, this jury was the first mixed jury in Plymouth Colony, as it contained six Native American elders. The three men were convicted and sentenced to be executed.

Soon after, Pokanoket warriors attacked Swansea, a small settlement in Plymouth Colony. They destroyed the small town, then came back later to kill and pillage some more. This was most likely done without the approval of Metacomet, but it is hard to know for certain since the Native Americans did not keep extensive records. Either way, Metacomet got the war he was looking for, as the attack on Swansea is considered to be the opening act of King Philip's War. After the attack, the Massachusetts Bay Colony's and Plymouth

Colony's governments decided to send a military expedition to a Wampanoag settlement in Rhode Island.

Just like the Pequot War, the colonial authorities sought the support of Native American tribes. In fact, during this war, the Pequots helped the Puritans, as did the Mohegans. This time around, the Narragansetts remained neutral, although a few of them did help out the Wampanoag Confederacy in some raids. The English sought more alliances, such as from the Nipmucks, but to no avail. When the colonists arrived at a Nipmuck village outside of Boston, all they found were empty wigwams, for the Nipmucks had already left to join Metacomet. Although the Wampanoags had a fairly large union of Native American tribes on their side, they were not truly united, and a number of Native Americans continued to cooperate with the English.

The initial military operations on both sides were spontaneous, and there was no organization. In the beginning, the war mostly involved the destruction of crops and the killing of cattle, but the clashes intensified in September 1675. This was perhaps due to the fact that the colonists officially declared war on September 9th, which would have undoubtedly kicked off more serious actions than punitive expeditions and raids.

Although comparisons can be drawn between King Philip's War and the Pequot War, there were some major differences. Unlike the Pequots, the Wampanoags had several fairly successful military actions, and they engaged in tactics that were more reminiscent of the English during the Pequot War. For instance, the Battle of Bloody Brook, which was fought on September 12th, saw a group of Native Americans attack a wagon train carrying food and supplies. The natives reportedly killed around forty soldiers and seventeen civilians. In October, right before winter, the colonial settlement of Springfield, Massachusetts, was burned to the ground, and although most of the people survived, the attack destroyed much of the saved food for the winter months.

In December, one of the harshest battles of King Philip's War was fought. Back in October, Plymouth Colony authorities had decided that some sort of action had to be taken against the Narragansett tribe. Although they hadn't truly participated in the war, they had given refuge to members of the Wampanoag Confederacy. The Puritans might have feared that the Narragansetts might join with the Wampanoag, which would have made the fighting even harder for the colonists. They also didn't quite understand which tribe was involved in the war efforts and which ones were not. Whatever the case might have been, the colonists decided to take preventive measures and burned several Narragansett villages in early November. In mid-December, Narragansett warriors attacked a Rhode Island garrison and killed around fifteen people. This prompted the largest military operation in the war to date. Like the Mystic Fort campaign, this campaign was reminiscent of those battles organized and fought on the European continent.

On December 19th, 1675, around 1,000 colonial soldiers and 150 Native American warriors marched toward Rhode Island to retaliate against the Narragansetts' attack. There, in the biting cold, the colonists and allied Native Americans surrounded the Narragansetts completely, without any possibility for escape. When they entered the fort, a great struggle began. Unlike the Pequots at Mystic Fort, the Narragansetts knew about the advance of the English troops, so they were ready to welcome the attackers. But they perhaps weren't prepared for the brutality that was about to be unleashed.

It is interesting that the crucial battles of both the Pequot War and King Philip's War involved the burning of a major fort. Just as at Mystic Fort, women, children, and warriors perished in the flames of the Narragansett fort. The exact number of causalities is not known, but it is believed that around 97 warriors and between 300 and 1,000 civilians died. However, unlike Mystic Fort, the Narragansetts were able to inflict some damage on the English ranks. Many Narragansett warriors fled the burning fort, and in the subsequent battle, around 70 English were killed and 150 wounded.

Throughout the winter, the Native Americans continued to use similar tactics as the ones used during the Pequot War, mostly employing guerrilla attacks. Unlike the Pequot War, most of these attacks were carried out on villages, meaning women and children were often victims. The natives avoided direct confrontation with the English troops rather skillfully. Due to the terrain, the British often did not have enough space for larger military maneuvers, with which they were most familiar. Most of the actual battles took place in areas like swamps.

The English tried to retaliate against these hit-and-run attacks, which led to one of the most brutal moments of the war, and this time, the English were not behind it. The Puritans had received information about the movement of Native American troops, and on March 26th, 1676, Captain Michael Pierce took about sixty colonial soldiers and twenty native allies to pursue the Narragansetts, who had just burned down several villages. Captain Pierce knew that the Native Americans favored ambushes and sudden attacks, but he must not have put too much significance on it. Even though he was an experienced soldier, Pierce made the mistake of acting hastily and abruptly mobilizing his troops without first observing the situation and sending a reconnaissance team ahead. As a result, the Narragansetts ambushed the English troops. The English and their allies formed defensive formations, but the number of English troops decreased as the battle progressed. The Narragansetts attacked in short intervals, which meant they preserved their energy while not giving their enemy enough time to take stock of the situation. The battle lasted a little less than two hours, and during it, nearly all the English soldiers were killed, including Captain Pierce. The Narragansetts, on the other hand, only lost a few warriors. The slaughter alone is brutal enough to place it in the history books, but the Narragansetts took it one step further. They took ten colonists as prisoners and then proceeded to torture nine of them to death. The site where the torturing took place is known as Nine Men's Misery, and one can still visit the plaque that marks the spot today.

King Philip's War continued throughout the summer of 1676, with the Native Americans being increasingly pushed back, although they did strike some severe blows. For the most part, though, they were on the retreat, looking for the perfect opportunity to gain a better foothold in the conflict. Unfortunately for them, that opportunity never arrived. In July, the female Niantic sachem, Quaiapen, went to retrieve food with a band of about 100 Native Americans. Around 300 colonists and 100 native allies attacked Quaiapen's force. Her men were destroyed, and those who made it out alive were sold into slavery. Quaiapen herself was killed in the clash, and many historians believe this was the point of no return for the Narragansetts, not just in the war but in general. After this, they would be unable to reorganize themselves efficiently, which led to the loss of many of their members. The Wampanoags also suffered, as they began losing allies left and right. It didn't help that the natives did not have the capacity or resources to continue the war against the English, who were much more sophisticated in terms of warfare.

The Native American alliance was dealt another great blow that summer when the sachem of the Narragansetts, Canonchet, died. He was captured by the English-allied Mohegan tribe and was executed. By August 1676, King Philip, or Sachem Metacomet, was constantly on the run. He was shot and killed by a man named John Alderman. Like John Sassamon, Alderman was a praying Indian. English tradition dictated that Metacomet's body be beheaded and then drawn and quartered. According to some sources, his severed head was placed on a stake, which remained in Plymouth for decades. Sources say that Alderman received Metacomet's head, as well as one of his hands, for killing the sachem. He later sold the head to Plymouth Colony for thirty shillings.

Metacomet's death signaled the end of the fighting in the main theater of the war, but the fighting continued in New Hampshire and Maine, the latter being a place where the Native Americans saw more success. The Treaty of Casco, which was signed in 1678, saw friendly relations being reestablished between the colonists and Native Americans, namely the Wabanaki. The English retained their right to the lands, but in return, they had to pay an annual tribute of a peck of corn for each family settled on them. Of course, since the Wampanoag had lost their war, they never saw a treaty that dictated friendly terms like this. However, many who had fought in King Philip's War in the southern theater made their way north to the Wabanaki. Today, one can find the descendants of these refugees living there. Some eventually returned to Massachusetts during the Seven Years' War.

Since the colonists were successful, they were able to acquire the land they had been seeking without too much resistance, at least for the time being. There wouldn't be another major war in New England between the colonists and Native Americans until 1722, with the outbreak of Dummer's War. However, massacres and raids still occurred, with both sides being the instigators. King Philip's War was important to the colonists in other ways, though. It marked the first large-scale conflict where the settlers acted on their own without any support from Europe. One could consider this the first stepping stone to the colonists realizing they could thrive on their own without European interference, although true independence wouldn't come to the colonists until a little less than 100 years after King Philip's War officially ended.

King Philip's War had dire consequences for the region. A large number of people were killed on both sides, and statistics show that when we look at the total population and size of New England, this was the most devastating conflict in the country's history. It is believed that around 5,000 Native Americans and 2,500 colonists perished. This equates to 40 percent and 5 percent of their population, respectfully. Many believe that, at the very least, it was the most devastating conflict in American colonial history.

In many ways, King Philip's War was reminiscent of the Pequot War. Both wars shared the same intensity of brutality, although the statistics are somewhat different. However, King Philip's War was a much larger conflict than the Pequot War, so it makes sense that the causalities would be higher. Many tribes took part, and this time, most of them sided with the offended Native Americans, unlike in the Pequot War, where the Pequots, for the most part, fought by themselves. However, like the Pequot War, many of these tribes suffered to the point where they couldn't find their feet again. For example, the Wampanoags were nearly wiped out to the point of extinction. After the war, it is believed there were only 400 of them left.

A key difference between the Pequot War and King Philip's War lies in the fact that King Philip's War was not a localized affair. The war took place in Massachusetts, Rhode Island, Connecticut, and even Maine. The war also caused enormous material damage. According to available information, by the beginning of the war, the British had founded about ninety cities in New England. The Native Americans carried out attacks on over fifty of them, seventeen of which were burned to the ground. The fact that King Charles II of England was aware of the graveness of the situation speaks volumes about the scale of the conflict, as the war significantly drained the financial resources of the colonies.

King Philip's War was novel in its own way, though. During the war, the English effectively disseminated propaganda. Bulletins appeared throughout England, especially London, showcasing the atrocities and brutal methods the Native Americans carried out against the colonists. The press closely followed the events in New England. For instance, an attack on an English family was carefully described. In this instance, a group of natives killed a family of six: a father, a mother, a son, the son's wife, and two young children. The details of that massacre were appalling to those who read about it, which further developed antagonism toward the natives.

However, like the Pequot War, there is a lack of written Native American testimonies. When scholars examine the events of the Pequot War, they are forced to use the narratives of the direct participants in the war, such as John Mason, John Underhill, and Governor John Winthrop, as Native American sources are almost nonexistent. The problem is these sources only reflect one side, so, inevitably, bias and distorted perceptions tint the writing. In such a situation, it isn't easy to make an accurate reconstruction of the events that took place, and the same was true of King Philip's War.

Early historiography transmitted information from the primary sources without a serious interpretation, ignoring the bias that might be present. After the Second World War, a new approach to the history of the Pequot War, as well as other colonial conflicts, was formed. Many newer-generation historians view wampum as the basic economic factor that led to the Pequot War. Several historians have also emerged who advocate the thesis that the English actions in the New World were directed against the indigenous tribes because of their greed; historians believe this was an effort to confiscate the natives' land and control the wampum, of which the Pequots had large stores. In addition to this, historians point to the cultural and social factors that led to the war. Religious factors, without a doubt, played a role in the outbreak of the conflict.

During the Vietnam War, there was a glorification of values, such as morality and the strengthening of liberal currents, in the United States. This was also reflected in the sciences and the interpretation of events in history. During this period, some American historians, such as Laurence M. Hauptman and Barbara Alice Mann, directly characterized the Puritans' actions, primarily the Mystic River campaign, as genocidal acts.

A more accurate insight of the Pequot War would be possible with the Pequots' testimonies, but unfortunately, none of those survived. In this way, history has been deprived of a complete picture of the Pequot War and the centuries-old relationship between the Native Americans and European immigrants.

Chapter 10 – Where Are They Today? A Look at the Pequots

By 1683, those Pequots who remained in the New England area were moved onto reservations. There weren't many of them left, as the vast majority had either been wiped out due to disease, the war, or had been made into slaves, with many of them being owned by those tribes who had helped the English. However, as time passed, some managed to make their way back to their ancestral home, and the government of Connecticut established two reservations: the Eastern Pequot Reservation and the Mashantucket Pequot Reservation.

It seemed as if the Pequots were losing the battle to keep their tribe intact as the years went by. As mentioned in an earlier chapter, a census in 1774 showed that there were 151 Pequots on the Mashantucket Reservation; by the early 1800s, that number had dropped to around 40. Many moved off the reservation, looking for work, and thus engaged in traditions that were more European in nature, such as attending English schools or converting to Christianity.

Take the efforts of Samson Occom (1723-1792) as an example. He was one of the founders of the Brothertown Indians, which was a Native American tribe composed of former members of the Pequot and Mohegan tribes, and they were firm believers in Christianity.

Occom himself wasn't a Pequot; rather, he belonged to the Mohegans, and it is believed he might have been the descendent of Uncas, the chief who separated the Mohegans from the Pequots. Occom's faith was unshakable, and he spent his life helping tribes like the Pequots assimilate into English culture, which included not only religion but also clothing, buildings, and food. However, even though Occom was a believer in assimilation, he was still treated wrongly by the English. For instance, around 1765, Occom reached an agreement with a minister named Eleazar Wheelock over the founding of a Native American school. Wheelock persuaded Occom to travel to England to gain more funds, and while Occom was overseas, Wheelock turned the school into Dartmouth College, one of the most prestigious universities in the United States today. But although Occom's dreams for a Native American school were dashed, his beliefs stood firm, and he continued to spread the message of Christianity throughout the area.

Occom's work was just one of the many factors that led to the dwindling numbers of the Pequots. In 1856, the state of Connecticut sold off a large part of the Mashantucket Pequot Reservation. The Pequots once lived in a space that consisted of 989 acres; now, they were reduced to eking out a living on a 213-acre-reservation. It is no wonder that many moved away, as the vast majority of the tribe migrated to the newly formed urban areas nearby, such as Westerly, Rhode Island. A census from 1910 states the Pequots on the Mashantucket Reservation only numbered around sixty-six.

In the 19th and early 20th centuries, many surviving Pequot members were forced to adapt to the new way of life that had sprung up in the country. Industrialization had transformed the country into a powerhouse, and these changes would not simply pass the Native Americans by. A large number of Native Americans were attached to the sea, engaging in the fishing and shipbuilding industries. Some of the Pequots earned their money from setting sail on fishing and whaling expeditions, which could last for months at a time. Besides fishing, the Pequots were also responsible for making sails and ropes to be used on the many ships docked in the harbors of New England. The practice of hunting whales had also intensified during this period. Whale fat, which would then be rendered into oil, was used for a number of things, including soap and cosmetics. It was a very demanding and complicated process to extract the desired whale fat, but some Pequots specialized in this business. Native Americans also helped produce harpoons and other equipment, and some of them even used their harpoons to earn a living. George, a Christianized Pequot, ran a specialty store in Mystic Harbor in the 1930s that manufactured barrels containing whale oil. In addition to this, there was an increase in trade, and the local ports formed by the English during the 19th century were a gathering place for not only the Pequots but also other members of descendants from the Pequot War, namely, the Narragansett and the Mohegan tribes. Women from the Pequot tribe were also involved in business practices, as they often rented out boarding houses to sailors from all over the world. Such circumstances allowed the Pequots to pass down their businesses and skills to future generations, which means that those who lived off the reservations would have no plans on returning anytime soon.

However, things wouldn't remain so bleak, although it took many decades for a resurgence to happen. During the 20th century, the Pequot community continued to be displaced from the Massachusetts area, mainly due to economic factors. The remaining Pequots in the area, whose numbers continued to fall, sought to live in harmony with the environment; to them, the land represented a crucial element of their tribal and individual identity. The 1970s was a decade of hope and promise for the Pequots, who began to move back to the Mashantucket Reservation. They realized that to have any hope of saving their culture, they needed to go back to their homeland and demand their rights. By restoring the land that had been illegally sold, the Pequots believed more members would come to join the tribe, and over time, they would be able to provide for themselves and develop their culture, which had been practically lost. If it wasn't for the efforts of these people, it might have been lost entirely.

The 1950s, 1960s, and 1970s proved to be a pivotal time for the Native Americans in general. Throughout history, there were many who spoke out about the injustices that had been done to them, but it was as if a switch was flipped in the late 1950s. More and more people engaged in activism to demand respect and recognition of their tribes be given to them. Militant groups also sprung up, demanding change, although this happened more in the late 1960s. And change definitely needed to be taken. In 1970, the Native American unemployment rate was ten times the national average, and around 40 percent of Native Americans lived below the poverty line. Life expectancy for a Native American was only forty-four years, and many of those lives were spent in squalor. The conditions on the reservations had deteriorated so badly that they resembled third-world countries rather than a part of the United States.

Different movements sprung up, and although each had different goals, a common ambition was the federal recognition of the lands that had been taken from them. They also wanted to be able to exert more control over their lands and have more of a voice in government. Although Native Americans had been designated as citizens in the 1920s, they weren't allowed to vote unless the state approved it. Their fight to vote carried on into the 1960s, and even then, this was hampered by poll taxes and literacy tests. This movement for Native American rights happened alongside the African Americans' civil rights movement, and both sides seemed to respect and champion each other's causes. Both African Americans and Native Americans wouldn't be guaranteed the right to vote peacefully until the Voting Rights Act of 1965 was passed.

The Pequots would join this movement for more civil rights. In 1973, the last remaining Pequot on the Mashantucket Reservation, Elizabeth George, died. Since no one was left living on the land, it was reverted back to the state of Connecticut, which happened according to the law. However, Elizabeth's family believed the land belonged to the Pequots, not the state. In 1975, Elizabeth's grandson, Richard A. Hayward, met with the Coalition of Eastern Native Americans, also known as CENA, and they helped him begin the steps to reclaiming the land. Richard also began campaigning for federal recognition of his organization, and a year later, Connecticut recognized his group, which he named the Western Pequots.

Richard and his group weren't alone in their fight. In 1976, the Pequots filed a suit against the landowners of the land that had been illegally sold in 1856 by the government of Connecticut. To help them win this battle, the Pequots gained the assistance of the Native American Rights Fund and the Indian Rights Association. They would fight in the courts for seven years until the land was finally given back to them. In the meantime, Richard Hayward and the Western Pequots were given a grant to develop an economic plan for the reservation, and they steadily rebuilt the small reservation so it met better standards.

In 1982, Hayward and his group sought federal recognition for a new tribe, which would come to be known as the Mashantucket Pequot Tribal Nation. However, in order to do so, they needed to get the Bureau of Indian Affairs involved. The problem was that the Western Pequots had no paperwork to prove their lineage, which they needed. In fact, American author Jeff Benedict believes the Mashantucket Pequots are not actually Pequots; his opinion is that they are actually descended from the Narragansetts. The Pequots have come out and stated that Benedict's assertion is false, especially since he fails to take into account the lineages of early 20th-century censuses, which shows the lineal descent of eleven Pequot families (this was used in the court case to prove their lineage). To push their claim through, the Western Pequots teamed up with the Pequots who were seeking to gain the illegally-taken land back. Although the bill passed the Senate, US President Ronald Reagan vetoed it, as he believed it would set an alarming precedent for the creation of tribes. However, members of Congress thought that Reagan had just passed over a bill that was of the utmost importance to saving Native American tribal communities. Reagan saw reason and came to a compromise, and the bill was passed later on in 1983. In addition to becoming federally recognized, the tribe was given enough money to buy back their confiscated land. It was a great moment for the Pequots because they were able to independently organize self-government and obtain certain legal powers. The federal recognition of the tribal community also granted the Pequots certain benefits in the form of healthcare and economic assistance for education.

The Pequots settled on the reservation and began finding ways to earn a living. Many became involved in selling maple syrup, cordwood, and crops. They also invested in pigs, a hydroponic greenhouse, and a sand and gravel business. Richard Hayward had grand plans of his own to revitalize the economy of the reservation, and one of the first things he looked into was building something that would make the reservation some fast money. He thought the best way to do this was to invest in a high-stakes bingo venture, which was opened in July of 1986. Two years later, it had generated over thirty million dollars.

That same year, the Indian Gaming Regulatory Act was passed, which set the framework for legalized gambling on reservations. Hayward realized that having a casino on the reservation would attract even more people, who would be encouraged to help the economy by supporting small businesses while in the area. However, many experts thought that this move was not financially viable because the Connecticut area was not a popular destination. Tribal representatives sent a letter to Wall Street, asking them to support their efforts financially. This request was not accepted, but the Pequot community did not give up. They sought financial help from a Malaysian investor named Lim Goh Tong, who was once the richest man in Malaysia. In 1992, Hayward opened the doors to the Foxwoods Casino, a world-renown casino today.

The casino didn't start out big, though. In the beginning, there were only table games, but slot machines were added about a year later. Although it wasn't a large enterprise in its early years, it held a monopoly on gambling in the region, which would allow it to expand even more since it had no other competition. Initially, the casino was intended to be opened for between eight and twelve hours. As time passed, and as the crowds continued to come, the owners realized they could stay open 24/7. Today, Foxwoods Casino has over fifty table games, almost 1,500 slot machines, a huge hotel, a 4,000-seat theater for concerts and the like, four restaurants, and four outlets. It earns billions of dollars in revenue, and it is the fourth-largest casino in the world.

In the Connecticut area, the Pequot tribal community is the largest private employer. In addition to the casino, there is a post office in that area called the "Pequot Post," which employs mostly members of the tribal community. The post office was opened in 1993, and since then, it has been performing standard tasks related to the mail. In regards to the post office, the tribal community repeatedly sought to obtain its own zip code, and their efforts finally bore fruit in 2002.

Today, the tribe can look back at its long history and see the tremendous strides they have made. Where they used to be only one member on the Mashantucket Reservation, there are now over a thousand. And instead of living in a territory that consisted of 213 acres, the Pequots now live on a reservation that covers a whopping 1,200 acres. It must be noted that there are more Pequots in existence than those living on the Mashantucket Reservation, although the exact number is not known.

Modern Pequots are constantly seeking to bring their history closer to the American people and their own traditions and culture closer to their own. They launched an initiative to increase the number of lessons about their history in educational institutions. To this end, they donated a large amount of written material, which is still waiting to be consolidated into one large study of the Pequots. The Pequots have also undertaken efforts to regain their language through these documents and through the analysis of closely related languages. They have reclaimed one thousand words so far, which is not enough to truly have a language of their own, but it is the start of something promising.

The Pequots managed to survive the turbulent times of history. It is a community that, at one point in its existence, almost faced extinction. But in the end, they survived the hardships that were placed before them.

Conclusion

The Pequot War represents one of the most significant episodes in the history of the United States. Before the war, the Pequots were a large community with thousands of members. They were the most powerful tribe in the wider Connecticut area, but with the arrival of the English, a new power would come to the forefront. But even before a shot was fired, the Pequots were decimated, like other tribes, by the infectious diseases the Europeans brought.

The Puritans' settlement of North America intensified during the 1620s. In the beginning, though, people got along peacefully enough. The English tried to be actively involved in trade, and due to this, they interacted intensively with the Dutch colonists and indigenous tribes, of which the Pequots were one of the most significant. In their search for commercial domination, the Puritans came into conflict with everyone. However, the Pequots also came into conflict with everyone as well in their quest to be the most dominant force, to the point where they alienated other tribes.

During the dramatic events of the 1630s, the Pequots killed English colonist John Stone. Almost no one was interested in the event at the time, but eventually, the Puritans would use his death as one of the reasons to start a war against the Pequots.

About two years later, John Oldham died, although who his murderer was is still unknown to history (although it is very likely it was the Narragansetts, who then framed the Pequots for Oldham's death). With these reasons in mind, the English felt they had no other course but to declare war upon the Pequots.

Many factors influenced the outcome of the Pequot War. The English won mainly thanks to their use of more modern warfare, their technological superiority, their organization, and their military tactics. The Pequots were inferior compared to the English when it came to those things, and since the English were still fairly new to the continent, the Pequots had not yet had a chance to study and learn the Europeans' way of fighting.

Without a doubt, the most important battle of the Pequot War was the battle of Mystic Fort. At Mystic Fort, the English killed between 400 and 700 Pequots, half of whom were burned alive. Most of the victims were children and women. With this campaign, the English prevented any recovery of the Pequot tribe.

John Mason sought to justify the massacre at Mystic Fort by using religion, which was a common justification back then. According to Mason, "But GOD was above them, who laughed his Enemies and the Enemies of his People to Scorn, making them as a fiery Oven: Thus were the Stout Hearted spoiled, having slept their last Sleep, and none of their Men could find their Hands: Thus did the LORD judge among the Heathen, filling the Place with dead Bodies."

Despite disagreements among historians about whether genocide took place or not, it is clear the war nearly wiped the Pequots off the face of the earth. The survivors were sold into slavery or given as gifts to the allied tribes. As a result, the English established total dominance in the Connecticut area. It was the first phase of the English expansion in North America.

In 1889, a monument to Captain John Mason was erected at the Mystic massacre site. Over time, initiatives have been launched to remove the memorial. This dispute became a long-standing problem for local authorities, and it was eventually removed and relocated to Windsor, Connecticut. The wider territory of the Mystic Fort is today in the National Register of Historic Places. It was added to that list on August 24th, 1979.

Here's another book by Captivating History that you might like

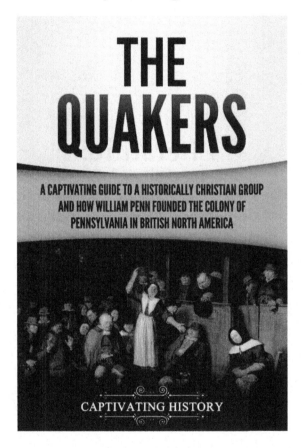

Literature:

Gary Anderson Clayton, "The Native Peoples of The American West: Genocide or Ethnic Cleansing?" WESTERN HISTORICAL QUARTERLY, Volume 47, Issue 4, Winter 2016

Michael Brown, *Shared History: Understanding the Impact of the Pequot War*, May 2016.

Bethany Berger, *Red: Racism and the American Indian*, University of Connecticut, 2009.

Alfred A. Cave, *The Pequot War*, University of Massachusetts Press Amherst, 1996.

Katherine A. Grandjean, *New World Tempests: Environment, Scarcity, and the Coming of the Pequot War*, Omohundro Institute of Early American History and Culture, 2011.

Denis Diderot, *Thoughts on the Interpretation of Nature*, France. 1754.

Raphael Lemkin, *Axis Rule in Occupied Europe: Laws of Occupation, Analysis of Government, Proposals for Redress*, Washington, DC: Carnegie Endowment for International Peace, 1944.

Philip Jenkins, *History of the United States*, originally published by Palgrave, Houndmils, Basingstoke, Hampspie, Beograd (Serbia), 2002, Translated by Filip Višnjić.

Jacobs Jaap, *Dutch Colonial Fortifications in North America*, New Holland Foundation, Amsterdam 2015.

Andrew C. Lipman, *Murder on the Saltwater Frontier: The Death of John Oldham*, University of Pennsylvania Press, Spring 2011.

John Lazuk, *Cultural Perception in Early New England: Europeans, Indians, and the Origins of the Pequot War of 1637*, University of Montana, 1983.

George Francis Dow, *Every Day in Massachusetts Bay Colony*, First Published in Boston, 1935 Reissued in 1967, by Benjamin Bloom, Inc. Reprint Edition 1977 by Arno Press Inc, November 2013.

Brenden Rensink, *Genocide of Native Americans: Historical Facts and Historiographic Debates*, University of Nebraska, Lincoln, 2011.

Group of authors: Kevin McBride, Douglas Currie, David Naumec, Ashley Bissonnette, Noah Fellman, Laurie Pasteryak & Jacqueline Veninger, "Battle of Mistick Fort, Site Identification and Documentation Plan," Public Technical Report National Park Service American Battlefield Protection Program, Mashantucket Pequot Museum & Research Center.

Group of authors: David Naumec, Ashley Bissonnette, Noah Fellman & Kevin McBride, "Technical Report Battle of Pequot (Munnacommock) Swamp, July 13-14, 1637," September 2017.

Group of authors: Allan Nevins & Henry Steele Commager, *The Pocket History of The United States*, Pocket Books Inc, New York, August 1992.

Primary Sources:

Lion Gardiner, *Relation of the Pequot Warres* (1660), University of Nebraska – Lincoln, Editor: W. N. Chattin Carlton.

John Mason, *A Brief History of the Pequot War*, University of Nebraska-Lincoln, Editor Paul Royster, August 2007.

John Underhill, *Newes from America; Or, A New and Experimentall Discoverie of New England; Containing, A Trve Relation of Their War-like Proceedings These Two Yeares Last Past, with a Figure of the Indian Fort, or Palizado,* University of Nebraska-Lincoln, Editor Paul Royster, August 2007.

Philip Vincent, *A True Relation of the Late Battell fought in New England, between the English, and the Salvages: With the present state of things there* (1637), University of Nebraska–Lincoln, Editor: Paul Royster, 2007.